which?

Make
the most of your
money

Many of us face unprecedented challenges when it comes to managing our money effectively and helping it grow. This book by Nic Cicutti aims to help you do that.

Nic Cicutti is an award winning personal finance writer and broadcaster. He has worked as a correspondent for the *Independent* and is editor of the *Financial Times* website, Ftyourmoney. Nic is currently special correspondent for Sky Money and writes for various publications including the *Daily Mail*, *Sunday Telegraph* and *Observer*.

which?

Make
the most of your
money

Nic Cicutti

- grow it
- save it
- spend it

Which? Books are commissioned and published by Which? Ltd,
2 Marylebone Road, London NW1 4DF
Email: books@which.co.uk

Distributed by Littlehampton Book Services Ltd,
Faraday Close, Durrington, Worthing, West Sussex BN13 3RB

British Library Cataloguing in Publication Data
A catalogue record for this book is available from the British Library

ISBN 978 1 84490 062 6

1 3 5 7 9 10 8 6 4 2

Although the author and publishers endeavour to make sure the information in this book is accurate and up-to-date, it is only a general guide. Before taking action on financial, legal, or medical matters you should consult a qualified professional adviser, who can consider your individual circumstances. The author and publishers cannot accordingly accept liability for any loss or damage suffered as a consequence of relying on the information contained in this guide.

Acknowledgements
Every book involves a huge collaborative effort. I therefore owe a big debt of gratitude to Claudia Dyer, who originally commissioned me, and Emma Callery, who made a silk purse out of a sow's ear. Also, apologies to our rough collie Sally, who again kept me company on this journey while pining desperately for a walk. Finally, Tina Campbell, who listened to my moans, read the raw manuscript, made useful suggestions and generally made me feel loved. She makes all the difference.

Project manager: Rochelle Venables
Edited by Emma Callery
Designed by Bob Vickers
Index by Lynda Swindells
Printed and bound by Charterhouse, Hatfield

Arctic Volume White is an elemental chlorine-free paper produced at Arctic Paper Hafrestroms AB in Åsensbruk, Sweden, using timber from sustainably managed forests. The mill is ISO14001 and EMAS certified, and has FSC certified Chain of Custody.

For a full list of Which? Books, please call 01903 828557, access our website at www.which.co.uk, or write to Littlehampton Book Services.
For other enquiries call 0800 252 100.

Contents

Introduction

If asked to think of a few words that we associate with money, there is a reasonable chance that many of us would say 'unease' and 'uncertainty'.

Sure, we appreciate the lifestyle it buys us, the many wonderful experiences on offer for those who have plenty of money and are willing to spend it. But when it comes to making decisions about how to look after our money, how to budget effectively, or how to grow the small nest egg we have into something significantly bigger, our attitude tends to switch, at best, to indifference – or, at worst, to suspicion.

In many ways, that is not so surprising. People often have a tortured relationship with money. We never seem to quite have enough of it and that lack, either real or assumed, makes us feel anxious. Spending it can sometimes serve as a short-lived cure for other dissatisfactions in our lives, while still making us feel worse afterwards.

Moreover, one of the striking things about the world in which we live is just how little control we appear to have over our money. The financial crisis that finally broke in the autumn of 2008 was the most obvious expression of this, with millions of us suffering the consequences in terms of rising unemployment, decimated pensions and other investments, much tougher credit conditions and an anaemic housing market.

The precise causes of what happened and who is to blame for the financial crisis we find ourselves in continue to be debated. Experts point to years of unbridled credit both here and in the US, of 'toxic loans' and of complex financial instruments no one understood as being at the heart of the problem.

Yet for many, the issue of who is at fault is almost irrelevant. It is the small daily indignities that have an equally disempowering effect: heavy overdraft fees on our bank accounts, mis-sold payment protection insurance, mystifyingly high credit card bills or the way the money we earn doesn't seem to stretch as far as it once did.

According to recent research by the insurer AXA, over 3.7 million people are failing to cope with mounting credit card bills and 1 million people have borrowed too much money and can't keep up with mortgage repayments. In all, around 11.6 million people – 25 per cent of adults – are struggling financially, with over half saying they have no savings left.

HOLDING BACK

The very scale of the problems means people are increasingly too scared to plan for their financial futures. According to research from CreditExpert, part of the credit rating agency Experian, three quarters of UK adults put on hold, or were planning to put on hold, key life decisions for 2009, such as moving jobs and even having a baby. Furthermore, over half (55 per cent) of all adults were feeling anxious about reaching their goals in life, mainly due to concerns over affordability.

What is increasingly clear from all the above statistics is that by the end of the first decade of the 21st century, a raft of assumptions we might have made about our finances no longer applies in the same way it did.

If asked back in September 2007, most of us would have assumed a continuation of what we had already experienced for at least a decade: full employment; decent education prospects for our kids; rising incomes; the availability of easy credit to finance a few small luxuries; a gentle but continuous improvement in our standards of living, buttressed by rising property and equity prices. Retirement, while not exactly comfortable, would be bearable financially.

Two or three years on, these are not things we can take for granted in the next decade or so. In effect, we need to look at planning our finances for a new era.

top tip: you can save hundreds of pounds a year by never automatically renewing any policy – car, household, life – when it falls due. Always shop around for a better one.

TAKE CONTROL

This book aims to help you take back control over your money. It looks specifically at the areas that most of us are finding difficult to deal with in today's tougher financial climate – and provides some solutions to those problems. For example:

- What financial goals do you set yourself?
- Where can you find the right advice you need?
- What kind of help can you get from the State?
- Is it still worth buying a property and, if so, how?
- How do you protect yourself and your family?
- What are the best ways to save?
- How do you reduce investment risk and keep hold of your money? Are there 'winning' tactics you can follow?
- How do you get out of debt and stay out of it for good?
- Are there still ways of keeping a chunk of your money out of the taxman's reach?

Each chapter in the book looks at one or more of the topics outlined above and offers guidance – and case studies – that can help you make successful financial planning decisions.

The interesting thing is that for some of us, this is a process that we have already begun. According to a survey by the Charities Aid Foundation in March 2009, three quarters of those questioned said they were thinking far more carefully about how they spent their money.

And despite the economic uncertainty, 77 per cent were giving as much to charity as before. When asked about how they viewed society today, compared to before the recession, a third thought that people are now more likely to help others in need. Nearly one quarter believed society was more caring and compassionate, with many of those questioned specifically thinking more about the needs of their immediate and extended family.

What this suggests is that financial planning and managing money more effectively is both about protecting and enhancing our lifestyles. But it also aims to help us feel better, by putting us back in control of our lives. This book aims to be your guide on that journey.

1: Financial goal setting

You know you need to do something about your finances, but you're not quite sure what. Time to sit down and work out a plan. This chapter looks at:

● **Goal setting and achieving**

Goal setting and achieving

Almost 160 years ago, Wilkins Micawber, a character in the Charles Dickens novel *David Copperfield*, uttered what has since become the 'Micawber Principle':

> 'Annual income twenty pounds, annual expenditure nineteen pounds nineteen and six, result happiness. Annual income twenty pounds, annual expenditure twenty pounds ought and six, result misery.'

Encapsulated in that single phrase is the essence of financial planning: if you have control over your money, how it is earned and how it is spent, you will be happy. Conversely, if you are unable to exert that control over what you earn and spend, the result will be misery.

But how does one achieve 'financial happiness'? The starting point is to set yourself some financial goals and then plan how to meet them. Financial goals are, in essence, the equivalent of a satnav device that tells you how to get to your destination and, if you take the wrong turn on your journey, will help get you back on track by mapping out a new route to travel on.

Like any satnav device, you need to plot exactly where you are going, decide when you want to start, whether you want to focus on big financial issues or are happy to take a less direct route to your goal – and also what other financial needs you may have along the way.

THE KEY INGREDIENTS OF EFFECTIVE GOAL SETTING

Again, as with a good navigation system, a goal needs to be specific; you need to know where you are headed, how far you have left to travel and how long it will take you to get there. You need to start by understanding the forces that may drive this process.

1 Be honest with yourself about where you are today. There is little point in setting a goal if you are unclear of what your current financial status is. For example, if you want to be free of your mortgage by the age of 45, you need to know exactly how much you owe now, what your current payments are and what your projected term is, based on current monthly payments.

2 Understand exactly what is involved. Goals are part of a dual process: you are deciding both a final outcome and the journey involved in getting there. In other words, they determine how you will live your life in the here and now and what your future will be.

3 Let your goals reflect your values. Goals that you set should be personal to you. They can be based on values such as honesty, status or security, for example. Without those personal ideals, a goal will have little meaning or relevance to you, making it much harder to try to achieve. Moreover, even if you do achieve it, it may hold less meaning to you than you thought. Establishing your values will also help you decide which goals are most important and worth working towards. For example, some people may decide on a goal of, say, having £1m in the bank by the age of thirty. They may be prepared to cut corners to achieve this goal. But to someone else with a different perspective, that much money holds no attraction. Reaching that £1m goal would only be seen as successful if the money is earned honestly, or according to a particular moral or ethical set of principles.

4 Goals are not just about money. For some people, money is not the only measure of achievement. Financial security need not be the same as wealth. Status is not the same as money – and some people may not want either in any case. So your financial goals may need to reflect more than simply being better off at some point in the future, or having more money available to spend.

5 Set out your goals in writing. Having a goal is one thing, making it happen is another. For most people, setting out their goals on paper helps clarify whether they really want it. It is also part of the process involved in working out how to achieve it.

6 Be very clear about your goals. There is no point in simply telling yourself that you want 'lots of money', or even that you want 'lots of money by a certain age'. Ideally, you should aim to achieve a very specific goal: 'an income worth £XYZ after inflation when you retire at 60', for example. That helps focus your mind on exactly what needs to be done to achieve it.

7 Understand your goals will have different end dates. Some goals may be short term and others need longer to achieve. Replacing your computer may involve finding £1,000 in a year's time, while planning your retirement could be a 30-year task. Distributing your emotional and financial resources between both short- and long-term goals needs to be carefully worked out.

8 Learn to prioritise between goals. Not all goals are achievable and trying to make impossible ones happen could be at the expense of others that are easier. This applies both to long- and short-term goals and their interaction between each other. For example, meeting an important long-term goal – being debt-free in 15 years – may mean downgrading a short-term goal, like going on a fortnight's holiday to the Bahamas next year.

9 Be prepared to compromise with others about your goals. You may have one set of goals, but your family may have another, or they may consider some elements of your goals to be more important than others. Or some of those goals may involve them, either in terms of an outcome or the journey you take to arrive there.

top tip: goals involve the allocation of human and financial assets – not always just your own: honest and considerate discussions among family members can reduce conflict over the use of resources to reach family and individual goals.

10 Goals are not set in stone. Instead, they are a dynamic process, in various stages of development, subject to change because of unforeseen events. You may need to adjust your goals to reflect what is happening in the outside world, or alter what you are doing to ensure your goal is reached. This means you should be prepared constantly to re-evaluate and review your progress so you will know when or where change needs to be made.

IDENTIFYING GOALS AND CHALLENGES

It could be argued that while we may plan ahead, any outcome is not just down to us but events that are unforeseen at the time the plan was first made. Yet it is just as often the case that plans fail not because of an unforeseen event, but because its likelihood, or its consequences, were not factored into the early planning stages.

For example, many life stages have important financial consequences, some desired and others not: such as leaving college, falling in (and out of) love, buying a house, having kids, losing a job, planning for retirement or needing long-term care. They need to be taken into account, some of them regardless of whether they actually happen. It is possible, for example, that the job you have is secure and you will never face redundancy. But experience suggests that such a view may, at times, be over-optimistic. If so, it makes sense to factor potential job loss into the goals you set, as they determine how much you may want to spend of your income right now and how much more you set aside for a rainy day in the event of something like this happening to you.

Similarly, many people assume they won't need to worry about long-term care after they retire. Yet research by the Rowntree Foundation shows that the number of people aged 65 and over in the UK is expected to rise by 81 per cent over the next five decades: from 9.3 million in 2000 to 16.8 million in 2051. The number of people aged 85 and over is projected to grow even faster: from 1.1 million in 2000 to 4 million in 2051, an increase of 255 per cent.

Of course, it is possible to create a financial plan that assumes you will not be in a position to meet the cost of long-term care if you should fall ill, in which case you would then be relying on the state or your family to provide that care – with all the consequences that flow from that decision.

The important thing is not necessarily that you have to try to save ever-increasing sums of money to pay for things that may or may not happen, like redundancy or long-term care. Instead, the goals you set yourself should flow from thought through assessments of what may be around the corner.

Set out your goals

Create a worksheet with column headings for 'Short-/medium-/long-term goals', 'Cost of the coal', 'Goal target date' and 'How much I need to save/find each month'.

Short-term goals have a duration period of six months to two years and could be to pay for a holiday, buy a car or replace a faulty boiler. Depending on how much you owe, it could also include reducing debt, such as cutting to zero how much you owe on a credit card.

Medium-terms goals apply for the next three to seven years, which might include raising the deposit on a property, repaying a large loan, setting aside a large nest egg for a designated purpose.

Long-term goals apply over ten years or more. Examples here might include paying off a mortgage, finding a lump sum to pay for your children to go through college or saving towards your retirement. Be specific in terms of what you want as that determines what you need to do in order to achieve that goal.

REACHING YOUR FINANCIAL GOALS

Once you have a basic roadmap of where you are and where you want to go, you need to break down your financial plan into a series of specific strategies that can help you reach that goal. What that means in practice is putting every element of your finances under the microscope

Set milestones

Setting milestones helps to measure what you are doing as well as setting realistic targets so you do not feel overwhelmed by the scale of the task ahead. For example, if a mid-term goal is to build up a £20,000 deposit on a home, you could break that into smaller sums of money: £5,000 after three years, £10,000 after five years and the remainder in eight years.

to ensure you are getting the best value for your money. Here are some basic things you will need to do.

1 Cut costs to create additional income. In order to save, you need to squeeze additional money from your income each month. This can be done either by cutting out things from your spending that you do not need or by paying less for the same things you were buying before (see page 62). Sticking to your budget will help you do this (see page 60).

2 Manage your debts. Many people assume that a central element of financial goal setting involves early repayments of a debt. That need not necessarily be the case: it is possible to use credit to bring forward spending plans for a time when they are needed urgently. The key is to make sure that you remain in control of your debts and that they are always affordable.

3 Invest your savings wisely. You need to have a clear understanding of the risks you are prepared to take with your money. For example, if you feel uncomfortable with the thought that your money can rise or fall in value over a period of months or years, sometimes very sharply, then investing in the stock market may not be appropriate.

But in turn, that also means that if you have a major long-term goal, such as retirement in 25 years' time, it may be necessary to revise estimates of how much you can expect your savings to grow each year. In turn, this either means you accept a smaller savings pot or set more money aside than you might otherwise have contemplated.

Take issues such as inflation into account. For example, if inflation is averaging 3 per cent a year, your investments need to return at least that much for your money to increase in value.

4 Work with a professional financial adviser. It is quite likely that there will be areas of your financial goal setting that require outside help. This is less to do with the actual goals themselves and more to do with talking to a professional who has an insight into the costs involved of various products that you may need in order to meet your goals (see page 21).

Case study

Ron is 55 years old, married with two adult children, has a salary of £40,000 and his wife doesn't work. He has a £40,000 mortgage on a £350,000 property, due to be repaid in ten years' time and no other outstanding debts. He saves £400 a month and has an emergency pot of £5,000. After discussion with his wife, Ron lays out the following short-, medium- and long-term goals.

Short-term goals	Cost of goal	Goal target date	How much Ron needs to save/find each month
Wedding of oldest daughter	£9,000	12 months	£333.33 (£5,000 already in savings account)
New central heating boiler	£2,500	18 months	£66 a month for 12 months, then approx. £280 a month for 6 months
Total	**£11,500**		**£400 a month for 12 months, then approx. £350 a month for 6 months**

Medium-term goals	Cost of goal	Goal target date	How much Ron needs to save/find each month
New extension to house (increased mortgage)	£20,000	10 years	Approx. £255 over 8 years at 5% interest rate (payments start after paying for wedding and boiler costs)
New car	£5,000	5 years	Approx. £145 a month loan for 3 years (after wedding and boiler costs are paid for)
Total	**£25,000**		**Approx. £400 a month for 3 years and then £255 for 8 years**

Long-term goals	Cost of goal	Goal target date	How much Ron needs to save/find each month
Boost pension income by £3,000 at age 65, rising 3% annually, with 50% spouse's pension if Ron were to die	£50,000	10 years	£370 a month (assumes annual fund growth of 6% after 1% fund charges, inflation of 2.5% and tax relief at lower rate)

By drawing up these tables, Ron can clearly see that he should be able to pay for his short- and medium-term goals by continuing to save £400 per month from his current account, or redirecting planned savings towards the mortgage, which he has increased by £20,000.

But when it comes to boosting his pension, this is likely to prove more difficult, as he will only have approximately £150 a month in available savings income for eight years before retirement in order to build up his pension pot.

Ron therefore decides to discuss his needs with an IFA (see page 23).

2: Planning your finances

You've thought about your goals and started to see how you can implement them. Now you need to take your planning further and consider getting some help. This chapter looks at:

- **Planning effectively**

- **Getting help**

Planning effectively

If someone were to propose a driving holiday to the south of France, the chances are that you wouldn't just leap into a car at the last minute and head off towards a ferry port without even booking a ticket first.

Depending on how organised you are, you might want to work out first when to go, how long for, where you are ultimately headed, how long it will take to go there and what your overall budget is. A truly methodical planner might even work out a daily itinerary, including mileage to be covered each day, which hotels or campsites to stay at and where to eat.

Regardless of where any of us sits within the spectrum, there is no doubt that planning can be enormously useful in most areas of life. Nowhere does this apply more than in the case of our finances.

Financial planning is not infallible. If you set out a series of goals based on projected life events – for example, buying a house at 35, paying for your kids' university education, or retiring at 60 – it will tell you what needs to be done to achieve those aims.

But as the recent recession shows, no plan can predict events in precise detail. You may be forced to redefine your goals and come up with new strategies to cope with events as they alter over time.

THE FIVE BASIC RULES FOR EFFECTIVE PLANNING
1 Start early. One of the vital lessons of planning is that the sooner you start, the less painful it will be in the long run. This isn't just for psychological reasons but straightforward financial ones.

For example, take planning for retirement. According to the Financial Services Authority's online calculator (see page 210 for details), if you are 25 and want a pension worth £10,000 in today's terms when you retire at 65, you will need to save £362 a month – before tax relief – for the next 40 years. By contrast, if you delay saving that amount of money by ten years, you would see the value of an annual pension fall to £4,392, less than half what the desired amount. (More information on pensions is given on pages 139–66).

2 Plan thoroughly. Financial plans that do not take a reasonable potential eventuality into effect can leave you unstuck. For example, it makes sense to plan for emergencies such as a redundancy, especially in the current climate.

It is also sensible to assume the possibility that future investment growth may not be as great as it was in earlier decades, or that property prices may not grow as fast. In turn, that can help determine how much you save, or whether you place as much reliance on the gains you can make by selling your family home and downsizing when you are close to retirement.

top tip: most of us think that the only thing we need in retirement is income. Yet as we live longer, the cost of care to help us live in our homes or to provide alternative accommodation becomes increasingly necessary.

3 Think laterally. Not every issue need have a straightforward or obvious solution. Nor is every potential issue easy to spot.

For example, many elderly couples assume that they need to plan their financial affairs in the most tax-efficient manner possible from the Inheritance Tax point of view. They understandably want to leave as much of their assets as possible to their beneficiaries, children especially, and avoid a large slice of that money falling into the hands of Her Majesty's Revenue & Customs (HMRC). But by preserving capital so that they can leave their assets behind, they may be reducing their overall income by a significant amount.

Rather than have this happen to you, an alternative valid option is to assume that you might live to, say, 90 years of age and so you can plan to gradually spend all the money over that period, including the capital. This means that in the early years after retirement most of your income would come from interest. As you get older, you would be spending more and more capital.

4 Talk to a professional. No matter how well we try to plan, the reality is that we are bound to miss something, either by failing to analyse a potential issue that needs to be addressed or not knowing the solution to that issue. Few of us will know all the answers to, say, HMRC's latest decree on Capital Gains Tax, or how to boost pension income. At such a time, it helps to talk to an expert who can give informed and dispassionate advice (see opposite).

5 Review all your decisions regularly. Often, the biggest problem that people face when it comes to financial planning is not that they fail to take every eventuality into account or that they made a mistake in terms of the plan they devise. The real failure is that of not updating the plan in the light of fresh circumstances.

This means you need to review regularly where you are going. With the best will in the world, a particular investment strategy may not deliver its stated aim. You may lose your job or your relationship may come to an end.

If so, it will be necessary to revisit your plan and decide what needs doing to get it back on track – or even to completely change it if that's what you want to do. In most cases, an annual review will do fine. Sometimes, you may need to look at things every six months or even more often if events are very fluid.

Getting help

Most of us are competent at making day-to-day financial decisions. But there are other areas where expert guidance is necessary. They may include protecting your family against sickness or death, finding the right mortgage, school fees or higher education planning and retirement planning.

Almost all of these areas are inter-linked. It is difficult to see how you can make a decision about one of them without it impacting on another, which is why you are likely to need expert help of some sort.

START WITH SOME RESEARCH

The best place to start is to do some of your own research. This book, newspaper or magazine articles and any further information you can glean from the internet are good starting points. There are many online calculators and websites that can help you make informed decisions about any of the above individual issues, as well as telling you about products you might wish to buy – or avoid – and why.

The challenge of doing your own research is that of making sense of disparate, often incomplete and sometimes inaccurate information, putting it all together and coming up with a financial plan that takes all aspects of your needs into account. For most people, that can be a challenge and so independent financial advice is often necessary.

THEN TURN TO AN ADVISER

Depending on what type of help you need, there are different types of adviser that you may want to talk to.

For advice on a mortgage

The most common sources of information tend to be lenders or mortgage brokers.

Lenders: These are usually only able to discuss their own range of products, which may not always be the most competitive. In addition, they operate under a set of rules set down by the City watchdog, the Financial Services Authority (FSA), which distinguishes between:

Giving full advice as to which is the most suitable mortgage.

Providing a customer with information so they reach their decision.

Acting on an execution-only basis, which means only providing you with the loan you asked for.

The difficulty lies in the first two categories, with some consumers believing that they were 'advised' while the lender operates on the assumption that it has simply handed over information enabling the decision to be made by the would-be borrower.

Mortgage brokers: These operate under the same rules, but you are almost invariably seeing a broker for his or her advice. Moreover, a broker will be able to tell you about more than one lender's mortgages, usually drawn from several dozen providers and sometimes right across the market. So you get more choice and a better chance of finding a home loan that suits your needs.

Many mortgage brokers are also financial advisers (see opposite). However, not all brokers who are also financial advisers are necessarily independent. They may have access to a wide range of mortgages but will be tied to a handful of companies when it comes to other products. So make sure you ask before taking their advice.

For financial advice

Typically, many people go to their bank or a similar financial institution for financial advice. Sometimes they go directly to a salesperson from a life insurance company that offers investment products.

The problem with this approach is that the bank or life insurance company employee's main focus is less on advice and more on sales. This is not always good: while many aspects of financial planning require a savings scheme to be set up, or a life insurance policy to be bought to protect a family, not all advice requires a sale to be made.

Furthermore, while most advisers are remunerated directly or indirectly by means of commissions on the products they sell, not all financial products pay commission, such as National Savings & Investments, which can mean they will be less likely to be recommended.

Independent financial advisers (IFAs): Using an IFA has several advantages compared to most salespeople: they are often specialists in various areas of financial planning or have access to others who are; and if a financial product is required as part of your planning needs, they are able to recommend one from the whole of the market, in much the same way as a mortgage broker. You can discuss investment strategies as well as make better financial decisions. Finally, an IFA ought to be reviewing your strategy with you to ensure that you are still on course to meet a goal and, if not, what you can do to make that happen.

Possibly the most important benefit of going to an IFA is that he or she is your agent. IFAs are are legally bound to act on your behalf, whereas life insurance salespeople are agents of the company that employs them.

Stockbrokers: If you are mainly a share-based investor, buying and selling shares on a regular basis, one option is to talk to a stockbroker. Brokers are able to act for you in one of three ways:

On an execution-only basis, where you tell them what to do.
On an advisory basis, where they offer recommendations but you make the final decision.
On a discretionary basis, where they are empowered to decide on your behalf.

Brokers are similar to IFAs in several respects: they give independent advice and are answerable solely to you.

Solicitors: Although solicitors are not automatically regarded as a first choice when it comes to financial planning advice, many do have financial advice qualifications and their knowledge of the law is often an asset, especially on issues such as wills and Inheritance Tax. They often refer their clients to financial specialists and even IFAs. But it is worth noting that this can be on a commission-sharing agreement. And just because you are referred to an IFA by a solicitor does not automatically mean the adviser is good.

Accountants: Another source of potential advice is the accountancy profession. Like solicitors, accountants are able to offer specialised guidance, especially on tax matters. And like solicitors, some do have additional financial advice and planning qualifications. Their practices may include an IFA division or they sometimes refer you to an adviser.

Wealth managers: These people specialise in investing your money and make all the decisions on your behalf. Wealth managers charge an initial fee of 1.5–2 per cent of total assets at the moment of investment, followed by an annual charge of up to 2 per cent. Some levy additional dealing costs of up to 1 per cent, but not on the entire portfolio: most would say they tend to buy and sell about a third of a client's portfolio each year.

The service is expensive, in that any growth must be at least that amount plus inflation in order to stand still. But wealth managers argue that they provide a specialised level of care for their investment clients, monitoring the performance of fund managers on their behalf and switching funds as necessary.

Inevitably, the service of a wealth manager tends to be restricted to investors with assets of at least £250,000.

FINDING AN IFA

Knowing that you need an IFA is a good starting point in terms of your financial needs. Finding one can be a challenge, however. There are several tried and trusted methods, but the truth is that not all of them are as effective as is sometimes claimed on their behalf.

Friends and family recommendation

This often figures high on the list of people's tips and it can be a good way of finding the right person. The difficulty with this approach is that not all your friends necessarily know what to look for in an IFA.

For a long time, especially when share prices seemed to be rising constantly, many advisers were able to bask in the fact that their investment recommendations appeared to be bearing fruit. As their clients' portfolios grew, the issue of why some performed better than others did not seem so important.

Neither did the fact that, quite often, some advisers rarely appeared to be reviewing their clients' portfolios on a regular basis, weeding out

top tip: before you make your relative's, colleague's or friend's IFA your own, always put him or her under the same scrutiny as the one you have found from any other source.

the poorer-performing funds and re-balancing all investments as and when necessary. Poor service seems to matter less when markets are rising. But when they fall, its absence will make a big difference.

Newspaper, magazine or news websites

This can be one useful way of finding a good IFA and works on the principle that if journalists, who presumably know something about the subject they are covering, keep quoting an adviser in their newspaper or magazine, then that individual must be good, especially if the adviser gets quoted often.

It is true that journalists will make a beeline for certain specialists and quote them approvingly. Often, the IFA concerned is genuinely good. However, this also presumes a number of things, not least that the journalist is as experienced as you believe; that the adviser is as knowledgeable as he or she is made out to be – and capable of delivering good service. Some advisers are good at delivering an instant quote to a journalist on a chosen subject and less good at serving their clients' needs.

Independent research

Doing your own research involves going to a number of websites and searching for advisers on the basis of several criteria – for example, if you prefer a female adviser, whether you need a particular specialism, or a commitment to ethical investments. There are a few websites that can help you do that, operated by different organisations all with a different stake in the advice process:

www.unbiased.co.uk is operated by IFA Promotion (IFAP), a marketing body that exists to sell the concept of IFAs to the general public. Its website has plenty of information to help you select an adviser.
www.searchifa.co.uk is run by a private company that IFAs register to join. You can search mainly on a geographical basis, although there are some advisers' details if you are looking for other specialisms.
www.financialplanning.org is offered by a professional body whose members focus more on overall financial needs than on specific financial product choices – although they also do that. They tend to offer a fee-based service rather than a commission-based one.

CHECKING OUT YOUR IFA

Once you have identified three or four IFAs, arrange to meet them and ask questions designed to provide you with the information you need to make a solid choice. Almost all advisers will let you have 30 minutes–1 hour of free time where you can ask them about how they operate. There are a number of things to look out for.

Qualifications

All advisers must have at least a basic qualification called the Certificate in Financial Planning. But many people believe it ranks roughly between a GCSE and an A level, so you should be looking for something better, if possible. New rules being introduced by the FSA are beginning to ratchet up the quality of qualifications needed by advisers. If you're not sure if these have yet been implemented, the IFAP website (see page 25) will tell you which exams come closest to your needs. For more details of qualifications to look for, go to www.which.co.uk/advice/financial-advisers/ifa-qualifications/index.jsp.

Having letters after your name is no guarantee of intelligence, professional ability or decent service. However, there is often a correlation between a good adviser and a commitment to learn as much as possible about a subject. Often, this expresses itself in a willingness to test this learning by means of various exams, which allow those who pass to claim designatory letters after their name.

top tip: don't expect your adviser to be an expert in everything, but he or she must be able to refer you to someone who is. Ask what the practice is in their firm.

Research and administrative support

Some financial advisers work from home. They do their own research, type their letters; a computer with internet facilities and a few software programmes is all they need to research the market and find the best deal. Face-to-face client meetings are usually held in your home.

Generally, however, a well-staffed research department with a range of analytical tools at their disposal will deliver more. Ask to be taken round the office. Try to strike a balance between outright luxury (who's paying for it?) and a comfortable and reasonably up-to-date environment.

Service

This is linked with the point opposite. Basically, if the adviser sees you just once a year, hands you a few bits of paper setting out the performance of your investments in the course of the previous 12 months and then recommends a new fund for your pension or ISA, you cannot be confident that your needs are being met.

What you ideally need is someone who can discuss your goals intelligently with you, who can bring together the various investments you have to meet that goal, while taking into account the different tax positions of each one. You need someone who can make planning suggestions that cover more than just investments (protection, banking, savings, mortgages, credit cards).

You also need them to provide you with a unified statement more than once a year showing where you stand in relation to any chosen goals and what needs to be done in order to meet them.

Alternatively, increasing numbers of advisers offer secure websites, accessed by their clients using passwords, where all this information is laid out and updated daily. More sophisticated sites even allow the client to create different scenarios, where they can calculate the effect of saving more or less money, or budgeting in different ways.

Either way, a good adviser should look at your assets at least every quarter, monitor their progress and call if necessary to recommend further action for you to take. Advisers earn an average 0.5 per cent commission each year on the value of your investments. That money is paid to service your account. They should be earning that money.

Fees or commissions

Your IFA is paid either through fees agreed directly with you, or by commission paid to your IFA by the company providing the product you purchase. It is up to you and your IFA how you choose to settle the bill. Your IFA will tell you up-front how he or she works. Some IFAs, for instance, operate only on a fee basis.

Paying fees: If you decide to pay a fee, you will know in advance what your IFA charges as an hourly rate. Be prepared to be quoted between £120 and £350 an hour for an adviser's time, probably plus VAT. Any commission paid by the product provider will usually be returned to you as extra policy benefits.

Paying commissions: Most IFAs are paid commission by the product provider, which they have to disclose. You should always be kept fully informed of the amount your IFA is earning before you sign on the dotted line. This is something you should automatically receive in plain and simple writing.

IFAs are required by their regulatory bodies to reveal how much they earn from commission when selling products such as investment bonds, pensions, savings plans and unit trusts. They are also obliged to give you suitable advice, so they have to look beyond the commission and take other factors into account – investment performance, charging

Case study

Jim Roberts, 53, and his wife Teresa, 47, are both in work. He earns £38,000 a year, or £2,335 a month net of tax. She earns £8,000 a year, £610 a month net. The couple have two children, John aged 17 and Josh, aged 12. The couple have a £120,000 mortgage on a £190,000 property, which they are repaying on a three-year fixed rate of 6.6%, taken out in July 2008. They now pay £1,070 a month. They own two cars, on which repayments cost £200 a month, plus a barely used motor home, costing them a further £175 a month over the next ten years. Other short-term loans for £6,000 cost an additional £300 per month – a total of £1,745 per month in debt repayments.

Teresa has never paid into a pension. Jim is currently a member of his company's money purchase pension scheme, into which he pays 6% and the company adds another 4%. His total pension pot is worth £28,000. Including a state pension, their combined income, will be about £10,000 a year in today's terms.

Over the years, they have paid into several tax-free ISAs now worth £7,500. Jim's employer offers no insurance in the event of his death.

In consultation with their IFA, Jim and Teresa came up with the following goals and plan.

Goals
● Jim and Theresa are not heavy spenders, but have made a few large purchases and their combined debt repayments take up 50% of their total take-home income, more than experts recommend. They would like to reduce this proportion significantly.
● The couple's two children are likely to be going to university in the next few years, one after the other. They would like to contribute towards both their children's university costs.
● Jim and Theresa have very little retirement savings and would like to build their pensions up further.

structures, your personal circumstances – before any recommendation can be made.

Commission is not necessarily bad. Although the suspicion of commission bias is often there, research by the FSA shows that it is not as great a likelihood as many fear. In some cases, paying commission may actually be cheaper than fees. Setting up a personal pension can take up to 5 hours, for example, so if you are only planning on making a relatively small monthly contribution you might pay less. If a company is offering a very high commission rate on a product, you may want to ask an adviser if he or she will take a smaller percentage of that commission, known as commission rebate.

Plan

- If Jim and Theresa were to try to redeem their existing loan and apply for a cheaper one, they would face redemption penalties of 2–3% of their mortgage – up to £3,600, plus they would be paying up to £1,000 in new mortgage charges. In this case, the costs would outweigh any savings, so a good financial planner would probably recommend that they stay with their existing loan.
- However, they could sell their barely used motor home for about £13,500, settling the remainder of what they owe on it.
- Although it is not always recommended, their independent adviser could arrange for them to increase their mortgage by £25,000, which would pay off the car loans and the short-term debts. If that tranche of money were placed on their lender's current SVR rate of 5.5 per cent for new loans, the additional cost would be £155 a month over 24 years.
- Taking these steps would reduce their debt repayments from £1,745 a month to £1,225, a saving of £520 each month.
- Jim and Theresa can use £250 a month – just under half the money saved – to make accelerated payments towards the £25,000 additional loan. Doing so would shorten the 24-year repayment period to six years, while their total monthly debt repayments would be £1,475. The remaining £250 a month can be used towards their children's university education.
- An adviser might suggest that the couple increase pension contributions, possibly by topping up Jim's existing pension scheme. This is because he may shortly go over the 40 per cent higher-rate tax bracket, which means his pension payments earn a larger rebate from HMRC. After both children have completed their university studies and the add-on £25,000 mortgage is paid, Jim and Theresa could redirect those funds towards a pension.

Fee versus commission: Some experts point out that if a person pays into a pension plan for many years, commissions based on total contributions made are more expensive overall. But most people tend to halt their pension contributions after a few years as their circumstances change – such as caring for children, buying a home or going through a divorce – and maybe start up again some time later, in which case heavy initial fees can be costly.

The FSA is currently consulting over plans to force IFAs to operate on a more transparent charging structure. From 31 December 2012, all IFAs will have to operate on a fee-paying basis or you may agree for them to be paid out of the charges levied on the product. But the exact amount you pay is up to you. The same, in theory, applies to annual renewal commission: the exact amount you pay is negotiable – and linked to the service your IFA is meant to be giving you.

Overall charges

All companies selling pensions, bonds, savings plans and collective investments must reveal their charging structures. These vary enormously from company to company. Your IFA will be able to explain how much a company is charging for investment management, and what the likely surrender values would be throughout the term of the policy (if there is one). (More details on charges are on pages 105 and 119.)

What does your adviser want from you?

Most clients assume that an adviser is simply there for them. But for an adviser to work effectively and deliver better value, he or she will need lots of information from you.

This means they need details about your finances, income and current spending pattern, your long-term goals, your family needs, whether you have any hidden ambitions and so on. For example, if you want to travel round the world for a year when you are 60, this is something an adviser can help you plan for financially – as long as he or she knows.

You need to be clear of where you stand in relation to things like how much risk you are willing to accept, the expectations you have of the IFA, including service, as well as the amount you want to pay. This has to be an honest relationship, where everything is discussed openly and in advance, otherwise it won't work successfully.

3: Maximising your earnings

Now that you are set up with an IFA, should you feel the need, it is time to start looking at how you can maximise your earnings. In this chapter, you will find out about:

- **Your financial rights at work**

- **Cutting your tax bill**

- **Tax: key dates**

- **Redundancy and insolvency**

Your financial rights at work

Over the years, workers in the UK have gained a series of legally protected rights as employees. Although it is not the scope of this book to discuss all of them, several are relevant to your financial wellbeing. Here are some of them.

PAY

You have the right to know what you will be paid, how often and when. This should be in the form of a written pay statement from your employer. The payslip should include:

What your wages are before any deductions.
Fixed deductions, such as trade union subscriptions, should be individually set out. Alternatively, an employer may choose to give you a so-called 'standing statement of fixed deductions' once a year, which sets out what they are, in which case you need only be given the overall total.
The individual amount of any variable deductions, for example tax.
Your wages (after deductions).

An employer can include additional information on your payslip, such as your National Insurance number, tax codes, the actual rate you are paid (annually or hourly), plus any additional payments like overtime, tips or bonuses, which may be shown separately. But this is not compulsory.

The National Minimum Wage (NMW)

The NMW is a minimum amount per hour which most workers over the compulsory school leaving age in the UK are entitled to be paid. The rate is reviewed every year and any changes take place in October, with different age groups entitled to varying amounts. All employers must pay the NMW to eligible workers – there are no exceptions for different types or size of employer. The rate is not based on geographical locations within the UK. In October 2009, the NMW is:

16–17 year olds: £3.57
18 –21 year olds: £4.83
Adults: £5.80.

Perhaps a more significant change is that from October 2010, 21 year olds, whose minimum hourly rate is currently the same as those in the 18-plus bracket, will be classed as adults and entitled to the higher rate.

What constitutes NMW? For many workers who are at or close to minimum pay limits, the issue of what does or does not count towards NMW is crucial. In addition to your basic pay, the following can count towards the NMW:
Sales commission, performance-related pay or other payments based on how well you do your job.
Tips, as long as they are paid through the payroll.

However, loans or special allowances, such as overtime or weekend working, or on-call payments do not count towards your minimum wage. So if your employer wants to add these to whatever else you are getting as part of your NMW, you are entitled to refuse it.

top tip: if you believe you are not being paid the NMW, you can call this helpline for advice on what to do next: 0845 6000 678 (Monday to Friday, 9am to 5pm).

SICK PAY

If you are forced to take time off work because of illness, you may be entitled to sick pay. There are two main types:

Statutory Sick Pay (SSP), which is a legal requirement.
Company Sick Pay, also known as Contractual or Occupational Sick Pay.

You are entitled to SSP if you are off sick for at least four days in a row (including weekends and bank holidays and days that you do not normally work) and if you earn more than £95 a week (since April 2009). The standard rate for SSP is £79.15 (May 2009).

Employers work out a daily rate of SSP by dividing the weekly rate by the number of days you'd normally work in that week. The 'SSP week' begins with a Sunday.

SSP is usually paid on your normal payday in the same way as your normal earnings and is subject to tax and National Insurance contributions – unless it is the only income you receive, in which case it may not be enough to pay tax on it.

Company Sick Pay schemes are more diverse in that they are offered at the discretion of the employer. But if the terms of a company scheme are set out in your contract of employment, that is what you are legally entitled to.

Although sick pay schemes vary from employer to employer, a typical one will usually take effect after a minimum period of service, for example a three-month probationary period. You would then receive your normal pay during any period that you are off work due to illness, up to a specified number of weeks.

When this initial period ends, you then get half-pay for a further period before any sick leave becomes unpaid.

Bear in mind that an employer is entitled to set out how you should tell them that you are sick. For example, you may have to ring in before a certain time of the day. Generally, a company scheme allows employees to self-certify – your calling in sick is taken on trust for a certain length of time. After that, you will need a sick note from a doctor.

HOURS OF WORK

An employee's working hours are usually set out in their contract of employment. However, they are also regulated by the Working Time Directive, whereby you should not have to work more than 48 hours a week on average, unless you choose to, or work in a sector with its own special rules, such as ship workers or senior managers judged to have control over their working environment. More information on all working hour issues is available from the Government website: www.direct.gov.uk.

HOLIDAYS

Although employers can offer generous rights in their staff contracts of employment, the amount of paid leave you are allowed is increasingly set down in law.

Since 1 April 2009 all workers have a statutory right to at least 5.6 weeks' paid annual leave if you work five days a week. Your employer can include bank holidays in the 5.6 weeks.

Employees start building up their holiday entitlements as soon as they start work and part-time workers are entitled to the same level of holiday pro rata (so 5.6 times your usual working week). Normal pay is payable while you are on holiday and you continue to build up holiday entitlement even while on maternity/paternity or sick leave.

PENSIONS

At a time when more and more attention is being paid to how the majority of the working population will be able to fund their retirement, any employer offering some form of occupational pension is worth considering very seriously.

In an occupational pension – of which there are two kinds: final salary and money purchase – an employer makes a contribution towards the retirement income of its employees. Occupational schemes are, in effect, a form of deferred income. For more information, see pages 145–51.

Other pension benefits

Quite often, employers will add other benefits to their staff's overall entitlements. For example, life insurance is quite often linked to staff's pensions. This can involve a payout worth between two and five times' annual salary in the event of the employee's death. This money is generally paid to the deceased's estate.

top tip: research a prospective employer's pension benefits when applying for or accepting a job offer. The difference at retirement can be as great as the ability to live fairly comfortably and being in long-term penury.

Other occupational schemes will pay an annual pension to the deceased staff member's family, sometimes going so far as to add a small annual amount for each child/dependent until they reach the age of 18 years.

OTHER PERKS OF THE JOB

Employers who are very keen to attract staff to join them may offer a range of extra 'bribes' to recruit and keep you. Among them are:

- Company car (see pages 43–61)
- Health insurance (see pages 83–4)
- Gym or health club membership
- Canteen
- Share save schemes
- Nursery vouchers
- Home relocation scheme.

All of these schemes have important benefits in terms of whether you should accept a job or otherwise. It is worth noting, however, that in some cases the offering of such benefits may also be liable to tax and National Insurance. This can be the case with company cars and gym membership, although not nursery vouchers or home relocation schemes up to a total limit of £8,000. The provision of canteens and even free or subsidised meals is not generally taxable as a perk.

INCOME TAX AND NATIONAL INSURANCE

Every person who works is potentially liable to pay a range of taxes, depending on what their earnings are. At its simplest, you pay Income Tax on your wages, business profits, if you are self-employed, and some State benefits, like Jobseeker's Allowance and Incapacity Benefit. In addition, you also have to pay National Insurance contributions (NICs).

If you are an employee, your employer will operate Pay As Your Earn (PAYE) and deduct tax and NICs from your wages before they arrive in your bank account. If you are self-employed, you are responsible for paying your own tax and NICs and filling in an annual self-assessment tax form.

Income Tax levels

There are three tax bands, plus an annual allowance on which no tax is paid. These figures are for the tax year beginning in April 2009:

- If you earn between £0 and £6,475, no tax is paid
- On the next £37,400, tax is levied at 20 per cent
- Thereafter – on incomes over £43,875 – tax is payable at 40 per cent.

National Insurance contributions

These are payable in addition to Income Tax and in the 2009–10 tax year, they are as follows.

Employees:
- If you earn above £110 a week (the 'earnings threshold') and up to £844 per week, you pay 11 per cent of this amount as Class 1 NICs
- If you earn above £844 a week, you also pay 1 per cent of earnings.

You pay a lower amount of NICs as an employee if you are a member of your employer's contracted-out pension scheme (see pages 143–44). Essentially, this means you receive a rebate of NICs in return for a smaller State Second Pension.

Self-employed: You pay two separate types of NICs:
Class 2 NICs at a flat rate weekly amount of £2.40.
Class 4 NICs as a percentage of your taxable profits – you pay 8 per cent on annual taxable profits between £5,715 and £43,875 and 1 per cent on any taxable profit over that amount.

2009 Budget

In his 2009 Budget, the chancellor announced a new top rate of Income Tax of 50 per cent, and higher NICs at 1.5 per cent without maximum limit from April 2010.

In addition, anyone who is earning over £100,000 will have part of their Personal Allowance – currently £6,475 – withdrawn. The clawback will cut Personal Allowances by £1 for every £2 of income above that threshold, which means anyone earning above £112,950 after April 2010 will lose all their Personal Allowance.

YOUR TAX CODE

When you start working, you are allocated a number based on your earnings, your employment status and family responsibilities – this is your tax code. The number basically reflects how much tax is taken from you and changes depending on how your circumstances change While it is easy to work out how much tax you should pay, potential deductions are determined by a range of additional personal factors.

The majority of tax codes are a combination of numbers and letters. Each number is used to work out how much income should be taxed, while the letter is used to determine how the income is taxed. The tax code also spreads your tax-free amount equally over the year so that you get about the same take-home pay or pension each week or month.

To arrive at your tax code, the following steps are taken:

1 Your tax allowances are added up. In most cases, this is just your Personal Allowance, but it may also include certain job expenses.
2 Income you have not paid tax on, for example untaxed interest or part-time earnings, and any other taxable employment benefits are added up.
3 The total income you have not paid any tax on (deductions) is taken away from the total amount of tax allowances. The amount you are left with is the total of tax-free income you are allowed in a tax year.
4 The amount of tax-free income you are left with is divided by 10 and added to the letter fitting your circumstances (see the table, opposite).

For example, the tax code 117L means you are entitled to the basic Personal Allowance. Then £1,170 must be taken away from your total taxable income and you pay tax on what is left.

Where to find your tax code

If you are employed or between jobs, you will find your tax code on your P45 (the slip of paper given to you by your employer when you stop working for them) and it is therefore very important to give your P45 to your new employer when you change jobs.

If you are starting your first job and therefore don't yet have a P45, your employer will give you a P46 form to fill in and sign instead. Your employer then allocates a tax code and works out the tax due. HMRC processes your P46 and, where necessary, revises your tax code.

top tip: you can also find your tax code on your PAYE Coding Notice, sent to you by your tax office, usually before the start of each tax year.

Common tax code letters

Letter	Reason For Use
L	For those eligible for the basic Personal Allowance – 647L for the 2009–10 tax year. It is also used for emergency tax codes, where HMRC has not yet decided how much tax you might need to pay
P	For people aged 65–74 and eligible for the full Personal Allowance
Y	For people aged 75 or over and eligible for the full Personal Allowance
T	If there are any other items that need to be reviewed in your tax code
K	When your total allowances are less than your total deductions (see How tax codes are worked out)
	If your tax code has two letters but no number, or is the letter 'D' followed by a zero, it is normally used where you have two or more sources of income and all of your allowances have been applied to the tax code and income from your main job or pension

If you have paid too much tax, your employer will make the necessary refund. (If the tax year has ended before this is worked out, then HMRC will make the refund.) If you haven't paid enough tax, your tax code can be amended to collect the underpaid tax. This happens in the current tax year, if there's enough time for your employer or pension payer to apply the revised code or, if not, in a later tax year.

It is also important to know that your tax code always depends on your personal circumstances. This means that if those circumstances change, you should always let the tax office know, especially if you:

Get married or form a civil partnership.
Separate and either of you were born before 6 April 1935.
Start to receive a second (or third or more) income. This can lead to people underpaying tax – and then facing a hefty bill.

If you don't tell HMRC, you could end up paying the wrong amount of tax. Similarly, if you believe that the tax code you are on wrong, make sure you contact your local tax office.

Cutting your tax bill

Few of us have any objection to paying a fair amount of tax. After all, everyone benefits in some small way from the taxes they pay, be it because they receive better health care, education, improved transport or policing.

Equally, the majority of us prefer to pay as much as we have to and no more. If there are ways of – legitimately – reducing the tax bill, we want to know about it. In fact, the many rules operated by HMRC offer taxpayers a range of opportunities to minimise their tax bill by claiming all appropriate allowances and exemptions.

IF YOU ARE SELF-EMPLOYED

When you are self-employed not every penny of what you earn is liable to tax. There are expenses relating to your work that can be deducted from your income. You then pay tax on the remainder. However, the emphasis is on legitimate expenses. This is not a way of avoiding tax by claiming unreasonable expenses. Remember that HMRC reserves the right to carry out an investigation into your tax return, so you must still keep any relevant paperwork for at least five years after the 31 January deadline of the tax year in question.

What count as allowable expenses?

Travel in connection with your work. This includes rail and bus travel, flights, petrol and maintenance on your car, plus any rental/HP costs on the car itself, parking and congestion charges (for mileage allowances, see page 46). If your car is also for home use, you must deduct the relevant proportion of any costs that were not work-related. Travel from

top tip: if you earn less than £15,000 a year, you do not need to itemise the expenses part of your tax form. You simply deduct the total from your income and pay tax on what remains.

home to work and vice versa is not deductible, but it is if you are visiting a client. You may be asked to produce a register of the work-related miles travelled. A chauffeur is also a tax-deductible expense.

Protective clothing used to cover your everyday clothing, but not that nice suit you bought to meet an important client. You would have to prove that the cost of the clothes has been 'wholly, exclusively and necessarily' incurred 'in the performance of the duties of the office or employment'.

Food and drink, although this is a thorny issue. You can claim subsistence while away from home, but not to extraordinary limits as this then looks like 'entertainment', which is not allowed.

Journalists are allowed to entertain contacts with a view to obtaining material or contributions from them. Clergy are also allowed to deduct the cost of 'reasonable entertaining' on official occasions, including for visiting clergy, officers of the church or members of church organisations.

Lighting, heating, phone bills, stationery (and tools), rent and Council Tax of business premises are all deductible, as is postage, cleaning, repairs, business-related insurance and similar expenses. But if you work from home, while you may be able to claim a tax deduction in respect of the room you work in, you may have to pay business rates on that part of the property and may also find yourself liable to Capital Gains Tax on the proceeds from that part of the house when the property is sold.

Training, such as professional courses, including travel to and from the course itself, and research trips – but don't confuse this with corporate hospitality: one-week 'seminars' in the Bahamas are out.

Membership of professional organisations – though trade unions are not usually allowable.

Items of capital expenditure, such as computers and software for professional use. Indeed, you may claim a 100 per cent allowance in the first year in which a computer was bought.

If your spouse helps you with your business, you can pay a reasonable amount for the work he or she does. Watch out for tax and National Insurance, as both may be payable. For the 2009–10 tax year if their salary (or that of any other employee) reaches £110 per week, they would pay National Insurance. If you pay someone £110 a week or more you will also have to pay employer's NI of 12.8 per cent.

Pension contributions, which are automatically topped up to the tune of 20p for every 80p you pay into your pension. If you are a higher-rate taxpayer, you can then claim back another 20p from HMRC. From April 2011, tax relief for those earning more than £150,000 a year will be reduced from 40 per cent to 20 per cent.

Case study

Martina Lukes, 36, is a freelance graphic designer. She has become self-employed, earning £46,000 in her first tax year. Martina has yet to complete her first self-assessment tax form. Although she will almost certainly be using an accountant for this, she'd like to know what her entitlements are, as well as what she might be able to claim relief on. Martina also wants to know if a pension makes sense for someone like her and if she can offset her evenings out against tax.

Goals

- Claim the maximum tax relief.
- Get tax relief from HMRC for entertainment.
- Investigate whether pension contributions make sense.

Plan

- Martina can claim for travel in connection to her work. This includes any train journeys, taxi fares, parking or congestion charges, as well as 40p a mile if she uses her car for work. Travel to and from home is not reclaimable unless she works from home.
- She is also able to claim for the cost of lighting, heating, phone bills, stationery and all equipment, as well as rent and Council Tax of business premises, plus any postage, cleaning, repairs, business-related insurance and similar expenses. This includes a 100 per cent allowance for her computer.
- Unfortunately, Martina will not be able to claim for going out in the evenings. She could try to claim a reasonable element of subsistence, but if challenged by HMRC, she would then need to show why such subsistence was necessary if the location she chose to eat/drink in was only a mile or two away from home.
- Pension-wise, Martina's gross earnings before expenses and reliefs is £46,000. This is £2,125 above the 40 per cent tax bracket in the 2009–10 tax year. Martina's pension contributions would receive relief at the higher level, but only in respect of that £2,125. Any contributions over that amount would receive relief at the lower 20 per cent limit. Moreover, if her accountant successfully claims additional tax relief so that Martina's gross income after expenses falls below £43,875, any pension contributions she makes will earn 20 per cent relief.

IF YOU ARE EMPLOYED

You may be entitled to a range of tax credits, benefits paid by the Government through the tax system. These include:

- Child Tax Credit (CTC) (see pages 77–8)
- Working Families Tax Credit (WFTC) (see page 78)
- Disabled Person's Tax Credit
- Child elements of Income Support
- Child elements of income-based Jobseeker's Allowance (income-based JA).

To find out more, check out HMRC's website: www.hmrc.gov.uk/Taxcredits/.

Expenses

Each year, along with your P60 employer's annual tax statement, you may receive another form called P11D, which lists the benefits and expenses incurred by you in the previous tax year. These may include:

- Company cars, vans and fuel
- Travel expenses and benefits
- Entertainment
- Childcare
- Medical insurance
- Loans, including season tickets
- Relocation expenses
- Living accommodation.

Check through the form to make sure that your employer has got everything right on it. If you are self-employed or have two jobs with separate employers, you will need to keep your P11D if you need to complete a tax return separate from the PAYE one already filled in by your employer.

Cars and motoring

Years ago, having access to a company car could be treated as a useful perk of the job. Today, the evidence increasingly is that company cars are no longer the wonderful draws they were even a decade ago. This is because company car drivers are now taxed heavily on a car, depending on how much it cost and how much it is judged to pollute the atmosphere.

In the past, company car owners were taxed according to how many business miles they drove each year. The more miles a company car owner drove, the less tax he or she paid. In recent years this has changed, so that you will pay tax if a company car is made available to you for your private use (this includes commuting) or you are provided with free or subsidised fuel for private use in that car. The tax you pay is broadly determined by three factors relating to the car:

- The list price, as set out in your P11D form
- The CO_2 emissions
- The fuel type.

top tip: the list price includes delivery charges, taxes, VAT, car tax, accessories (such as a CD player), fitted before it was delivered, and accessories costing over £100 that were fitted after it was delivered.

The normal charge is 15–35 per cent of the list price of the car, though the reductions for cars with low CO_2 emissions or alternative fuels can reduce the charge to below 15 per cent. Most diesel-fuelled cars incur a 3 per cent surcharge to reflect their greater adverse effect on air pollution, but the charge still won't be above 35 per cent.

The tax system is designed to favour cars that are less damaging to the environment and encourage you and your employer to choose such cars. The CO_2 output of a vehicle is also a deciding factor in the eventual benefit in kind – as the CO_2 increases, so does the benefit in kind payable. Cars that can run on alternative fuels such as hybrid electric and LPG also have reduced tax charges.

If you only have access to the car for part of the tax year, the car benefit is reduced in proportion. So if you actually have the car for only five months, your car benefit will be 5/12 of the total. If the car is off the road (perhaps because it has broken down) for more than 30 consecutive days, it is reduced in proportion to the number of days.

Tax charges on a car based on CO2 emissions

% of P11D price to be taxed	CO2 (g/km) 2009–10	CO2 (g/km) 2010–11	CO2 (g/km) 2011–12
10*	120 or less	120 or less	120 or less
15*	135	130	125
16*	140	135	130
17*	145	140	135
18*	150	145	140
19*	155	150	145
20*	160	155	150
21*	165	160	155
22*	170	165	160
23*	175	170	165
24*	180	175	170
25*	185	180	175
26*	190	185	180
27*	195	190	185
28*	200	195	190
29*	205	200	195
30*	210	205	200
31*	215	210	205
32*	220	215	210
33**	225	220	215
34***	230	225	220
35****	235	230	225

* Add 3% for diesel.
** Add 2% for diesel.
*** Add 1% for diesel.
**** Max charge, so no supplement.
To find out what your car's CO2 emissions are, go to: www.vcacarfueldata.org.uk.

How does the CO2 emissions table work in practice? Here is an example based on the information given above:

In 2009–10, a new Ford Focus ECOnetic 1.6 TDCi 5dr, with a P11D price of £17,705 and CO2 emissions of 114g/km, would attract a tax charge of 13 per cent of its P11D value: a 10 per cent charge plus the extra 3 per cent diesel surcharge. £17,705 x 13 per cent gives a taxable value of £2,302, equating to yearly tax liability of £460 (£38 per month) for a 20 per cent taxpayer or £921 (£77 per month) for a 40 per cent taxpayer.

Employees using their own transport

	First 10,000 miles (per mile)	Thereafter (per mile)
Car/van	40p	25p
Motorcycle	24p	24p
Bicycle	20p	20p

Mileage allowances

If you drive your own car for work reasons, either as a self-employed person or as an employee, you will want to make use of mileage allowances, approved rates at which anyone in the UK using a private vehicle for business journeys can claim tax-free expenses for that journey. They are as shown above.

Income Tax and NICs are due when allowances exceed these rates. Employees can claim tax relief on any shortfall. Rates of up to 5p per mile, per passenger, are also tax and NIC free when paid for the carriage of fellow employees on the same business trip.

Free fuel

Employees with company cars who are given free fuel or who are reimbursed by their employers for fuel that they use for private motoring also have to pay a tax charge. To work out whether this is to your tax advantage, you must work out what mileage you would achieve by 'paying' for the free fuel through your taxable benefit.

The taxable benefit that occurs when an employer provides an employee with fuel for private motoring is calculated by applying the same percentage figure as for the car benefit – that is, to reflect the car's CO_2 emissions – to a fixed figure set by the Government: £16,900 in the 2009–10 tax year.

How does this work in practice? Take a Ford Mondeo ECOnetic Estate 1.8 TDCi (125PS). It has CO_2 emissions of 142g/km and combined fuel consumption of 52.3mpg (11.51 miles per litre), which means that its tax percentage is 19 per cent in 2009–10.

The fuel scale charge is therefore £16,900 x 19 per cent = £3,211, equating to an annual fuel tax liability of £642 for a 20 per cent taxpayer, or £1,284 for a 40 per cent taxpayer.

Assuming the price of diesel at £4.66 a gallon (102.5p/litre), £642 will pay for 137 gallons/625 litres of diesel for a 20 per cent taxpayer (or 275 gallons/1,250 litres for a 40 per cent taxpayer).

Break-even mileage would therefore be 7,165 private miles (137 x 52.3) for a 20 per cent taxpayer, or 14,383 private miles (275 x 52.4 = 3) for a 40 per cent taxpayer.

Therefore, if the number of private miles you cover is less than the calculated figure, consider paying for your private fuel yourself as it will cost less than the tax you pay. If the number of private miles you cover exceeds the calculated figure, you are better off paying the tax.

Cash or pay for it yourself?

Some employees may be lucky in that they have a choice between taking a cash payment from their employers instead of the car, or a car allowance. Which is the best option?

As always with tax, it depends on your personal circumstances. You need to look at the monthly allowance on offer, deduct tax and NICs and add in the monthly tax saving from not having a company car.

You can then calculate whether the remaining sum will be enough to cover your motoring costs, including depreciation, servicing, insurance and so on. The best way to do it is to test it in practice.

top tip: there are many online calculators to help you decide, including one from the AA. You can find it at www.theaa.com/motoring-advice.

Tax: key dates

Paying tax involves meeting a series of deadlines every year, which apply to the tax declarations you need to make, as well as to the payment of bills. Here are the most common deadlines for 6 April 2010–5 April 2011. They work both in arrears and in advance. For example, by 31 January 2010 you would have had to submit your return for the tax year ending 5 April 2009, as well as finish making payments for that year.

HMRC send you an initial assessment based on your previous year's declared earnings. If you believe that your earnings will be below the previous year's, you can ask for the amount to be lowered by requesting to pay in less, although you risk a fine if you get it wrong.

6 April 2010
This is the date the new tax year starts. A 2009–10 tax return or Notice to Complete a Tax Return (SA316) is sent out to all people who get a tax return each year.

There is also an investment deadline relating to 6 April. The previous day – 5 April – is the deadline for investing your annual limit in a tax-free Individual Savings Account (ISA), in an Enterprise Investment Scheme (EIS) or a Venture Capital Trust (VCT) for 2009–10. Also, 5 April is the deadline to invest up to your maximum annual limit in a personal or stakeholder pension for the tax year just ended.

31 July 2010
The deadline for paying an instalment 'on account' of personal tax for the 2010–11 tax year. The payments are due on 31 January in the tax year and 31 July following the tax year.

31 October 2010

The deadline for submission of your paper-based 2009–10 personal self-assessment tax returns to HMRC, for those who are self-employed or may have an additional tax bill to pay, such as Capital Gains Tax (see pages 194–8). If you submit your return by then, your tax office will:

- Calculate your tax
- Tell you what to pay by 31 January 2011
- Collect tax by amending your tax code, instead of demanding a large lump sum, in cases where you owe less than £2,000.

If you fill and submit in your tax return online, your tax liability is automatically calculated for you.

31 January 2011

The final online deadline for submission of your 2009–10 self-assessment tax return, with the tax due calculated by you or your accountant. If you fail to send in your form by this date, you will automatically be fined £100.

By this date, you must also pay the balance of any 2009–10 personal tax you still owe, plus the first instalment for the 2010–11 tax year must be paid by this date.

1 February 2011

Interest on any overdue tax (the balance on your 2009–10 tax year, plus the first instalment on 2010–11) starts to accrue.

28 February 2011

If your personal return is still outstanding, a further penalty of £100 or any tax owed, whichever is less, is imposed. Plus, an automatic 5 per cent surcharge is levied if you have failed to pay your 2009–10 personal tax by this date.

6 April 2011

The new tax year starts. A 2011–12 tax return or Notice to Complete a Tax Return (SA316) is sent out to all people who get a tax return each year.

Redundancy and insolvency

In the first three months of 2009, it was reported that almost 5,000 companies were declared insolvent, meaning that they did not have enough money to pay the people they owed in full.

At such times, people's jobs – perhaps yours – are under threat, especially if a business cannot be sold by a receiver to another interested party. Even if it is, redundancies can still happen. Indeed, they can happen whether a firm is declared insolvent or otherwise.

So what are your monetary entitlements if this happens to you?

REDUNDANCY

You have the right to a redundancy payment if:

You are an employee who has worked continuously for your employer for at least two years and you are being made redundant, or
If a fixed-term contract of two years or more expires and is not renewed because of redundancy.

You do not have to claim this money from your employer, they should automatically pay it to you. Some employers offer employees more generous packages than the statutory minimums as part of their employment benefits.

Your employer cannot offer you less than the statutory minimum through your employment contract. The total amount you should be paid for redundancy is based on how long you have been continuously employed, your age and your weekly pay, up to a limit of £350. Basically, you are entitled to the amounts of pay outlined on the opposite page.

0.5 week's pay for each full year of service where your age is under 22.
1 week's pay for each full year of service if you are aged 22 or over, but under 41.
1.5 week's pay for each full year of service if you are 41 or older.

INSOLVENCY

The insolvency practitioner, appointed to oversee a firm's affairs during this period, will normally send you the necessary forms for claiming any money you are owed.

Because there is no guarantee that all the debts can be met in full, there are special arrangements to ensure that anyone affected receives a basic minimum of the debts owed from the National Insurance Fund (NIF). These debts include any:

- Redundancy pay owed
- Wages owed
- Holiday pay owed
- Basic awards for unfair dismissal
- Unpaid pension contributions.

This is all payable by the Insolvency Service's Redundancy Payments Office. Separately, HMRC is responsible for unpaid Statutory Sick Pay, plus maternity or paternity (and adoption) pay.

What you can claim for

If your employer is insolvent, you can claim:

- Redundancy
- Wages owed (up to a maximum of eight weeks)
- Holiday pay owed (up to a maximum of six weeks)
- Notice pay.

top tip: if you don't receive the relevant forms, the HMRC claim forms are available at any JobcentrePlus office, together with further advice on other entitlements.

Although you can claim for any of these elements, you are not guaranteed to receive them. For example, any pay owed after you have already received a payment from the NIF will become payable only if there are enough funds left after the company's assets have been counted up.

Some debts, including holiday pay and wages, are treated as a preferential debt when those are shared out.

If you and other employees have been paying into a pension scheme at work, the pension fund trustees can apply to the Secretary of State for some of your employer's unpaid contributions to be paid into the scheme.

Notice pay

You can claim one week after one month's service, rising to one week per year of service up to a maximum of 12 weeks. The maximum week's pay you can claim for is £350. This includes commission, overtime and other guaranteed payments. It also includes statutory payments for time off work or suspension for medical or maternity reasons.

4: Credit and debt

This chapter explores the credit and debt options available, both for those who want to find the best available deal and those who want to keep a tight rein on their spending and pay off what they owe. It also offers help to those who are feeling overwhelmed by debt and want to know how to budget more effectively.

- **Credit rating and how it works**

- **How to budget effectively**

- **Dealing with bad debt**

Credit rating and how it works

To help you establish why your application has or has not been turned down, it is important to understand how credit rating actually works.

THE CREDIT SCORING SYSTEM

Before they agree to lend money, issue a new card, finance a hire-purchase (HP) deal or even let someone have a new mobile phone, all providers go to one of three main credit reference agencies to find out more about their applicants.

The agencies collect a wide range of information about every adult in the UK, all 35 million or so of us. This information is culled from a variety of sources, such as the electoral register and other credit providers, who feed data on their borrowers back into the system.

That information – hundreds of millions of disparate elements of information supplied annually – is then collated by the credit reference agencies and supplied to potential lenders on request. In turn, the lenders use the data as the key ingredients they feed into the scoring system they use when considering credit applications.

The amount of potential information held about you is vast. For example, it may include:

Your name together with anyone else on the electoral register living at the same address. This information tells a lender that you are who you say you are, whether you have moved between addresses and even if you are linked with other people who have credit problems themselves.
All your credit agreements – mortgages, loans, credit cards, HP – even mobile and landline phone bills, plus details of any late payments and defaults. This information about you can be held for up to six years.
County Court Judgements and bankruptcy orders against you. These

are also held for six years and, along with information on whether you have discharged those debts, are obviously a key determinant in terms of whether you are likely to be seen as potentially reliable.

Previous applications for credit. If you get turned down more than a couple of times, this is known as a 'footprint'. Some potential credit providers view such footprints negatively: they start to wonder why you might have been turned down. Or rather, they may have programmed their credit scoring software to reject applicants with multiple footprints.

IMPROVING YOUR CREDIT RATING

The most important thing to understand is that credit scores held about you are never static. They can change regularly, depending on what credit-related activities you are engaged in.

For example, if you didn't pay a mobile phone bill nine months ago but your repayment history has been spotless since then, your credit score will probably be assessed more highly than someone who missed two payments in the past six months.

This is why, if you are turned down for credit, it is easy to get upset or to imagine that nothing can be done. In fact, there are many things you can do.

Check the information held on you

The Data Protection Act of 1998 entitles you to know the information in your credit report and, where necessary, challenge its accuracy. If you want to do this, send your name and address, together with a cheque or postal order for £2 and a list of your previous addresses over the last six years, to each of the following credit reference agencies:

CallCredit: Consumer Services Team, PO Box 491, Leeds LS3 1WZ
Equifax: Credit File Advice Centre, PO Box 1140, Bradford BD1 5US
Experian: Consumer Help Service, PO Box 8000, Nottingham NG51 5GX

Although credit providers will generally only use one of the three agencies in question for their data, all three will hold almost identical information about you. For example, if you apply for a Barclaycard, while it may use just one reference agency to check your record, any subsequent decision is then communicated to all three agencies, hence the need to write to all of them.

Correct any inaccuracies

If there is a mistake on your file, you cannot simply ask for it to be corrected by the reference agency itself. You must contact the organisation that provided the information and get them to acknowledge that the information it has supplied about you is wrong or inaccurate. For example, if there are entries that involve credit account information (lenders or credit card issuers, for example), that is who you should talk to. The reference agency itself can help with details, including an address.

Once you have that information, here are the steps to follow:

1 Write to that organisation/credit provider. Ask it to correct any incorrect details about you and to inform the credit reference agencies. You will have to provide a written reason, with a factual explanation for that organisation to correct any wrong or misleading information about you. Once that organisation has done, the information will generally take between two to four weeks to be updated across all three agencies. Experts suggest you might want to check again to make sure they have done so.

2 If necessary, add a Notice of Correction. If the financial company or credit reference agency is unwilling to change information about you because it is 'factually based', you may add a 200-word statement to your credit file (the Notice of Correction), to explain any entry on it.

Bear in mind that if you add a Notice of Correction, lenders searching a credit reference agency's database for information held about you are obliged to read it. This may slow down their decision of whether to offer you the product or service you have applied for.

3 If necessary, obtain a Certificate of Satisfaction. If you have failed to pay a bill, the organisation you owed money to may have gone to a County Court (Sheriff's Court in Scotland) and obtained a judgement against you, ordering you to pay. This is known as a County Court Judgement, or CCJ (a Decree in Scotland). You may then have settled that debt. But details of that CCJ will be on your credit file.

If you have paid off that debt, contact the County Court and ask for a Certificate of Satisfaction, which will cost you £10 and confirms that you have paid the debt. Send it to the credit reference agencies concerned.

4 If necessary, add a Notice of Disassociation. If there are entries on your personal file that relate to a family member, partner or someone else living at your address and you have had a financial relationship with them in the past, this notice breaks the link between you and anyone else at the address who may have a poor credit history. You will need to write to each of the three credit reference agencies, obtain your credit report from them, then write back with the information that disassociates you from any individual named by you. The agencies have 28 days in which to place the Notice of Disassociation. If they refuse, they must tell you why, normally because you have failed to send in something they have asked for. If they refuse, you can raise a complaint with the Information Commissioners Office to enforce them to place the notice. This can take about three months.

Pay off and reduce your bills and debts

Some people believe that as long as they pay their regular bills on time – the mortgage, personal loans or HP agreements – their credit score will be good. Or that simply missing one or two payments, for example, on a mobile telephone bill, is unlikely to have a significant impact on their credit scores. In fact, that is not the case – or at least, not any longer. Here are the four key things you need to remember:

Pay ALL your bills on time. Late payments can have a negative impact on your rating.
If you have missed payments, get up-to-date and stay up-to-date. The more you pay your bills on time, the better your rating becomes. Likewise, the longer you keep making regular payments, the better your credit rating will become.
If you are having trouble making ends meet, contact your creditors or see a credit counsellor. The Citizens Advice service in your area will help (www.citizensadvice.org.uk). This may not improve your credit rating immediately, but if you can begin to manage your credit and pay on time, your rating will improve over time.
Try to pay off debt rather than move it around. For example, it may seem clever to constantly shift your debt between 0% credit cards (assuming you are able to obtain more than one of them), but, in fact, it does not work: a credit search will show that you are a multiple card applicant, which will lower your credit score.

Note that although unpaid credit and CCJs remain on your file for six years, they are marked as settled as soon as you pay the debt. This is often taken into account and works in your favour when making future applications.

Build a credit history

One of the reasons why many people get turned down for credit is that they lead blameless financial lives – which, in turn, means that there is not enough information held about them for a lender to make a decision on.

In such cases, it is often easier to turn an application down rather than take chance on an 'unknown' applicant. So if you always pay your bills on time, never borrow money, don't use a credit card and only have one bank account, it means when a credit check is carried out, there's nothing there for a credit provider to see whether you would be a good or a bad credit risk – so you get rejected.

Conversely, there is nothing lenders or credit card issuers like better than a good credit record where borrowers show they can successfully repay amounts they owe and manage credit and debt. How do you deal with this? Here are four key tips to remember:

Ensure you are on the electoral roll. Lenders always check the electoral roll to confirm your name and address, so make sure you have registered to vote. If you are eligible to vote, you can register at any time by filling in a registration form and sending it to your local electoral registration office, which is usually at your local council office. You can download a form from the About My Vote website (www.aboutmyvote. co.uk) or your council website.

Apply for a small overdraft on your account, maybe even a small loan. Pay it back as agreed.

Apply for a credit card. Successful applications could be seen as a sign of credit-worthiness. Just apply for one, though, because every time you apply for credit it is registered in your file, which will be seen by other lenders and issuers. A large number of searches over a short period could signal financial over-commitment or even fraud. So you may decide that it is more sensible not to apply for a credit card until absolutely necessary.

Your credit footprint

Following on from the footprint issue, not all credit is 'suitable' for all borrowers. Credit providers tend to target different market segments and you may not find out a lender's particular lending approach or how they score you until after you have applied for a loan. If you are rejected, you risk leaving a footprint on your file.

However, for a fee, all three main credit reference agencies offer a rough-and-ready points-based assessment of your rating, which you can then use to apply for credit from the 'right' provider. This reduces the chance of being turned down for credit. Some price comparison websites also allow you to see what loans you are most likely to be suitable for.

Be honest when you apply for credit

Faced with the possibility that they may be turned down if they disclose financial problems, some would-be borrowers think they can get away with not being completely honest in their applications.

This is a mistake. Credit providers use automated systems to trawl through an applicant's personal financial history, all of it culled from a credit reference agency. This may literally take seconds and, in the process, any discrepancy or omission will count against an applicant.

Therefore, avoid the temptation to be half-truthful when applying for credit. If you have moved around a lot in the last three years, don't leave out any previous addresses. This could be seen as an attempt to conceal unpaid credit at that address and treated as suspicious.

Also, be honest about your credit history. If you have been in difficulties in the past and been unable to meet your repayments, or you have got CCJs, make sure you tell your prospective lender.

How to budget effectively

While credit can be an effective financial planning tool for many, managing our finances more effectively is very much part of the same process. Controlling what you spend and how you do it, paying off debts regularly and getting the best value for your money is the reverse side of the same coin.

If you can budget effectively, it means you need to borrow less. You pay less interest on your debts and can afford to either spend or save more, depending on your personal financial goal. The challenge, as ever, is that of how to make it happen.

PREPARING A BUDGET

The simplest place to start is to look at your bank statement. This will tell you two things: how much you earn every month and how much you are spending. There are several online calculators that can help, including one from the FSA. You can find it at: www.moneymadeclear. fsa.gov.uk/tools. But it is also easy to do it on paper.

Necessary items of expenditure

Here are the main expenses you should be able to work out:

- Rent/mortgage
- Council Tax
- Commuting
- Gas

- Electricity
- Water
- Telephone bills (including mobiles)
- Food
- TV licence.

Apart from food, each of these items is likely to be a fairly predictable amount and most are payable by standing order or direct debit.

Irregular items of expenditure

The next element of spending consists of items that we are likely to face from time to time rather than every month, such as:

- Car and household repairs and maintenance
- Dentist and optician bills
- Insurance, such as car, home contents.

Less necessary items of expenditure

You could probably do without these if you are looking to make economies:

- Going out/entertainment (drinks, films, clubs, restaurant meals)
- Smoking
- Newspapers or magazines
- Coffees to and from work
- Canteen at work
- Sweets/chocolates/crisps and other 'treats', such as the hairdresser
- Unnecessary food
- Unnecessary clothes
- Holidays and weekends away.

Most of this spending will also be in your bank statement and some may be set down in your credit card bill. A few items are bound to be one-offs and you will need to add them up and divide by 12 and then add to the above listed areas to give you an idea of how much you are spending – on average – each month.

CUTTING YOUR SPENDING

Once you know what you are spending every month, you can then begin to cut your expenses. There are essentially two main ways.

Maintain the same lifestyle but look for cheaper ways to do it

That means seeking out better deals on just about everything, including insurance, energy bills and so on. Shopping around, in other words.

For example, make sure you are getting the best deal on your fuel and that you are on the best tariff. Often you can get further concessions if you obtain your gas and electricity from the same supplier – a facility known as 'dual fuel' deals. You can also get further discounts by paying by direct debit and opting for paperless billing.

Consider switching to metered water if your consumption is low – quite likely if you live alone or are there are just two of you in the house. Check out bundled packages for television, broadband and telephone, to see if you can save money by switching. While you are at it, consider if you really need one of the more expensive packages anyway.

Doing without things

For example, you might consider setting yourself a fixed weekly or monthly budget and not spending beyond that limit. You might want to peg your food shopping to £60 a week or spend no more than £100 a month on clothes.

top tip: create separate 'jars' or 'envelopes' into which you put money every month or week. If you take money out of one, you have to make up for it by economising from another jar.

Dealing with bad debt

Many borrowers, particularly those in financial distress, are unaware of what alternatives are open to them, such as negotiating with creditors or getting help from free debt counselling services. There are other options, too, such as debt consolidation, Administration Orders or an Individual Voluntary Arrangement (IVA).

NEGOTIATING WITH CREDITORS

Even though we do our best to control our spending and to work within a tight budget, for some people, debt can become a serious issue, in which case they need more help than simply advice on how to budget more efficiently.

1 Admit you have a problem. Often, people deny they are in trouble. They ignore letters from companies they owe money to, or throw away their bank statements without opening them. In some cases, they may even carry on spending more money rather than face up to the need for help. In all such cases, the starting point for dealing with the issue is to be completely honest with yourself.

2 Calculate exactly how much you owe. Another common problem that those in debt have is that they don't know exactly how much they owe. This can be because the debts are spread around many sources: credit cards, loans, bank overdrafts, HP agreements, even friends and family. But the only way to deal with debts effectively is if you know the full extent of the problem. Don't ignore those debts where the creditor appears to have gone temporarily silent.

3 Stop saving money. It is possible to be in debt while still saving small sums of money every month. Yet the interest paid on any savings is almost certainly lower than the rate of interest charged on most loans, mortgages and credit cards. Moreover, interest paid on savings may be taxed for those in work.

4 Ask for your money back. This may include debts owed to you by family or friends, tax overpayments, even unfair bank charges. If you have become unemployed, make sure you are claiming all the benefits and allowances due to you, including Jobseeker's Allowance. Claim fare and entrance concessions and free prescriptions if you are entitled to them.

5 Work out how much you can afford to pay back. Experts suggest a rule of thumb for this is that an absolute maximum of 50 per cent of monthly net income should go towards paying back any credit you have taken out, such as credit cards, loans, a mortgage, overdraft and HP deals on a car. In addition, no more than 20 per cent of take-home income should go on other standing bills, such as utilities (water, electricity, gas, telephone), TV licence payments. This may not seem like much, but the rest of your income needs to go on other regular household bills, plus food, travel and so on. If you have children or other dependents, the amount you can pay back will be less.

6 Prioritise your debt payments. Start by protecting the roof over your head. This means placing your rent or mortgage payments first in the queue. Then come bills where you risk going to jail or being fined in court if you don't pay up. This includes council and other taxes, including Income Tax or your TV licence. Non-payment of Council Tax means the money may be taken from your wages or benefits. Fuel debts, because you face disconnection for non-payment, and HP on essential items should also be given top priority.

If the sums you owe are relatively small and do not involve secured debts, it can make more sense to pay off the most expensive debts first. For example, a credit card generally charges a higher APR than a bank loan: it therefore makes sense to reduce payments towards the loan and focus on repaying the credit card debt first.

Primary and secondary debts

If you need help deciding what is a primary debt (one that needs to be paid as a matter of priority) and a secondary debt (one that is less urgent), the Credit Action website (www.creditaction.org.uk) has an impressive list of debts that can be classed in both categories, along with explanations of why.

7 Negotiate with your creditors. Now you can contact each creditor and make an offer of repayment, depending on their importance in your plan and how much you can offer to pay. You should find most creditors will be anxious to strike a deal. At the end of the day, they know that if they don't, they risk the possibility of you not paying their bills at all.

Often, the temptation is to refuse to answer calls from creditors, or to duck out of sight if they knock on your front door. Among the many factors that can influence creditors' decision to pursue a debtor is if there is no communication between both sides. This sometimes leads to more aggressive and intrusive attempts on their part to recoup their money. Keeping them informed is part of the process of ensuring that harassment is kept to a minimum.

However, talking to creditors is not the same as allowing yourself to be intimidated by them or their agents. The Office of Fair Trading (OFT), the credit watchdog, has produced guidance that sets out the types of debt collection practices that it considers to be unfair. To find out more, go to: www.oft.gov.uk.

8 Get expert help if you need it. Organisations like Citizens Advice (www.citizensadvice.org.uk) have helped thousands of people like you. The Consumer Credit Counselling Service (CCCS) charity will also help (www.cccs.co.uk). What they do is start by working out what you can agree to pay each week or each month, then help divide that amount between all your debts.

top tip: never pay for debt counselling or any firms that claim to be able to help sort out your debts. They are charging you for free advice – and they may not be able to help anyway.

9 Stick to any agreements you make. If you agree a repayment schedule, you should stick to it. There's nothing more guaranteed to make creditors go mad than someone who goes back on a deal. Don't think that making a deal with creditors will be plain sailing: you will be expected to make certain personal sacrifices in order to pay back the money you owe. If so, use the section on budgeting (see pages 60–2), to help you make necessary cuts in your spending.

10 Avoid falling back into the same trap again. There is no point in reaching an agreement with creditors if your spending remains out of control. This is the time to rein in your spending.

Some people find that simple, if dramatic, gestures such as cutting up all their credit cards and paying for everything in cash help them to

---

Case study

Mary Franks, 26, earns £23,500 a year, or £1,551 a month net of tax. Her rent is £650 a month and travel to work costs £120 a month. Other household bills – landline telephone, mobile, gas, electricity, council tax, water, television licence, car and home insurance – add up to £250 a month. She also spends £400 a month on 'treats', which include coffees at work, lunches, going out, clothes and holidays.

Mary has debts of £27,000, including £21,000 on several credit cards, on which she is repaying a minimum 5 per cent, or £87.50 a month; a three-year £4,500 car loan, taken out 12 months ago, being repaid at £150 a month; plus a semi-permanent £1,500 bank overdraft, on which she pays interest charges of £20 a month.

Her income more or less matches her expenditure – except that her credit card debts, on which average interest of 17.9 per cent APR is being charged, are growing faster than she is paying them off. Currently her credit card debt is growing by more than £2,700 a year.

Goals
- Get Mary to accept that she has a serious financial problem.
- Pay off her debts within 5 years.
- Ensure she does not return to the same situation in a year or two's time.

Plan
- Cut up all existing cards and live only off earned income.
- Shop around for better deals on some of her necessary expenditure: home insurance, telephone and mobile (if absolutely necessary), saving £30 a month.

---

budget more effectively – the logic being that using 'real' money instead of a plastic card provides a more realistic understanding of what you are spending. It also means that you have to have the funds necessary in your bank account to withdraw the money in the first place, or negotiate an agreed overdraft.

DEBT CONSOLIDATION

In recent years, the idea that it is better to replace different debt repayments, all with varying rates of interest and payment periods, with a single monthly repayment – debt consolidation – has become a popular way of dealing with debt. The advantages of debt consolidation can be lower interest rates, lower monthly payments and dealing with only one creditor. However, there are disadvantages too (see overleaf).

- Stop most 'treats', saving £300 a month (to deny all rewards could be counter-productive, so leave £100 to be used as Mary wishes).
- Create budget, in which specific sums of money are allocated to individual spending needs.
- Sell the car and use the proceeds (£2,500) to reduce Mary's most expensive credit card debt.
- Focus on Mary's current debts: her credit cards. Enter into an agreement with her credit card companies, so that no further interest is added to existing debts. Use Citizens' Advice Bureau to negotiate the deal.
- Ask her loan provider to agree a temporary £50 a month reduction in loan payments, without adding interest to debt, or extend the repayment period by one year, leaving three years to pay.
- Increase card repayments to £450 a month, focusing on the most expensive card first, then directing sums to lower interest-charging cards as appropriate.
- Annual repayments of £5,400 in first year would mean repaying card debts (now £19,000 after sale of car) in four years or less, but in Year 2 it may be a good thing to reduce debt payments slightly – by £30 a month or so and using that extra money as a 'reward' for showing such repayment discipline – and again in Years 3 and 4.
- Redirect surplus cash to car loan repayment, as necessary.
- Do not apply for any credit cards or loans in the first four years. Thereafter, stick to one card only.

The costs of settling an existing loan, such as redemption penalties, and arranging a new one can be significant.

Loan providers have tended to add payment protection insurance (PPI) to the loans they make, sometimes without borrowers understanding what they are paying for.

Using one of the other ways of dealing with bad debt, such as an Administrations Order or an IVA, might be more effective for your circumstances.

ADMINISTRATION ORDER

If you have a number of small debts, up to a maximum of £5,000, you can apply to the County Court for an Administration Order.

This is a court order whereby you make a monthly payment to the court, which then distributes that money on a pro rata basis among your creditors. The court takes 10 per cent of your payment as handling fees to cover their costs, which they deduct directly from your monthly payments. There is no application fee.

While the order is in place, no creditor included in the order, without the leave of the court, is allowed to take action against you. In addition, debt collection procedures and letters against you are stopped.

To apply, you must have at least one CCJ issued against you and at least two creditors. Form N92 for applying for an Administration Order is available from your local court. On it, you will be required to list all your debts.

Where there are debts with joint liability (where two or more people are jointly responsible for all the debt) and several liability (where each party is only liable for its own share of that debt), you should include the whole amount. However, even if finances are shared, couples cannot apply jointly and must make separate applications. Where a couple each make individual applications for an order at the same time and theirs is a joint debt, it may be acceptable to divide the debt equally between the two applications.

For employed applicants, an Attachment of Earnings Order will be made, where a proportion of their income will be automatically deducted by their employer, unless they specifically request otherwise on form N92. Since many debtors do not want their employers to know of the situation, most debtors prefer not to have such an order.

If you do not maintain your payments, the court can revoke the order. Your creditors would then be entitled to pursue you for the full amount owed to them. Should you feel that you cannot afford to pay the amount stipulated in the order, perhaps because of a change in circumstances, you can ask the court to review the order and reduce the payments.

Once you have paid off your debt under the order, you can obtain a Certificate of Satisfaction (see page 56) from the court. You will have to pay a £10 fee for this certificate.

INDIVIDUAL VOLUNTARY ARRANGEMENT (IVA)

In recent years, IVAs have become a common – if occasionally controversial – mechanism for people to deal with their debts. Essentially, an IVA is an agreement to pay back a certain amount of money to creditors, though not the full amount owed, at a set rate each month, over a certain number of years. At the end of that time, the debt is judged to have been settled in full. For people burdened with heavy debts, IVAs have several advantages:

You may only pay back a percentage of your debts.
You only have to make one monthly payment or, in some cases, a one-off lump sum.
The IVA is legally binding so that your creditors cannot change their minds once they have agreed.
You can have a bank account as long as it does not have an overdraft facility.
It may safeguard your property – although creditors will almost certainly require savings and realisable assets, such as endowment policies, premium bonds and ISAs, to be cashed in.
It does not affect the ability for you to hold public office or your professional status.

If you feel an IVA is right for you, contact an insolvency practitioner (IP), who will negotiate with creditors on your behalf. The trade body is the Association of Business Recovery Professionals, or R3. It has lists of members in each region and can be contacted via its website (www.r3.org.uk).

Your IP will ask about your current financial situation and agree a repayment amount with you. You must sign this agreement. The IP then

The rules in Scotland: Trust Deeds

Scottish law is slightly different. In Scotland, in place of an IVA you have a Trust Deed, which is a legally binding agreement between an individual who is unable to pay his/her creditors and a licensed IP (the trustee, in this case). The trustee puts together a form of proposals to the creditors for approval and, if agreed, then administers the Trust Deed. Provided certain conditions are met, the Trust Deed may be registered as 'protected', preventing creditors from taking further steps – such as sequestration (the Scottish term for bankruptcy) – to recover debts due to them.

makes an application to a court for an Interim Order, which states that you are working to achieve an IVA. Once this is in place, no creditors can take legal action against you.

Creditors meeting to approve the IVA

Your IP will arrange this and you should attend it, too. For an IVA to be approved, creditors vote either for or against the arrangement. If creditors don't vote, it is assumed that they are in favour of the IVA. However, if just one creditor votes against the IVA and he or she represents less than 25 per cent of your total debt, the meeting is suspended until a later date and other creditors who did not vote will be called upon for their vote. If the creditor who voted against the IVA represents more than 25 per cent of the total debt you owe, the IVA fails. This is because IVA can only ever be approved if 75 per cent in monetary value is voted for. In the case of a consumer IVA, creditors or their representatives rarely attend the meeting as most prefer to vote by fax or by post.

Payments

Most IVAs are generally based around a regular monthly payment over 60 months. As long as you keep up the repayments, when the term of your agreement is finished, you will be free from these debts regardless of how much has been paid off. During the period of your arrangement, your financial situation is reviewed regularly to see if there has been any change in your circumstances.

Under the terms of an IVA, it may feel that you are paying nothing to the IP who has done the work. In fact, he or she is taking a cut of your monthly payments, with fees ranging between 15 and 20 per cent.

The potential downside of IVAs

In recent years, the growing role of IVAs has drawn controversy, largely because although their proponents have portrayed them as a simple process that allows people to get creditors off their backs while only paying a fraction of what they owe, for many people, the reality is anything but. The important point to realise is that for an IP to get all creditors to agree to an IVA, he or she has to promise to extract the maximum possible amount from you. Moreover, any money the IP earns is dependent on how much you pay.

In addition, many IPs will be dealing with the same creditors – banks, credit card issuers, HP firms and so on – on a regular basis. To maintain the creditors' trust in the process, the IP can't be seen to go easy in terms of how much you are asked to repay.

As a result, many people who take on an IVA find that they have to make much larger payments than they might have anticipated. Furthermore, some of them are forced to declare themselves bankrupt after two or three years, as they are unable to keep up their regular monthly payments – albeit that part of the issue for some is that they have not been able to control their old spending habits.

BANKRUPTCY

Bankruptcy proceedings aim to free you from overwhelming debts so you can make a fresh start, subject to some restrictions (known as Bankruptcy Restriction Orders (BROs)), while also ensuring that your assets are shared out fairly among your creditors.

A bankruptcy petition is usually presented at the High Court in London or a County Court near to where you live or trade and a first-time bankrupt is discharged from his or her debts and released from restrictions after a maximum of 12 months. Where cases are administered quickly and creditors agree, this period can be reduced.

Bankruptcy in Northern Ireland and Scotland

A similar procedure to that of England and Wales applies in Northern Ireland. In Scotland, where bankruptcy is known as sequestration, you have to go through a Sheriff's Court, which will order that both debts and assets of a person should transfer to an appointed trustee.

This applies to bankrupts who have failed 'through no fault of their own' and who co-operate with the authorities. That said, 'dishonest, reckless or blameworthy' bankrupts could face restrictions for up to 15 years, while BROs bar people from obtaining credit without disclosing their status, trading under a different name or holding a company directorship for between 2 and 15 years. The Insolvency Service decides, on a case-by-case basis, if a BRO order should be pursued through the courts.

The drawbacks of bankruptcy

Despite the easing of rules concerning bankruptcy, there remain important disadvantages to this course of action. They include:

You may still lose any assets of real value, including your home, vehicle, investment policies, life insurance and possibly some pension entitlements (if it is deemed you paid excessive contributions to avoid that money being handed over to your creditors). You might be able to keep your vehicle if you can prove you can't do your job without it.

While you are bankrupt, any assets you acquire – such as inheritances insurance settlements or wins on the Lottery – will be taken away from you.

Your building society, landlord and all other creditors will be informed immediately of your new status. Bank accounts will be frozen, credit cards taken away, some HP agreements will be ended and many of your possessions taken away and sold.

If, or when, your bank unfreezes your accounts, you won't be allowed a chequebook or an overdraft until the bankruptcy is discharged. You will also find it difficult to open a new bank account elsewhere.

You cannot obtain more than £500 of credit without declaring that you are an undischarged bankrupt. To do so is a criminal offence.

You may lose your job and will certainly not be able to practise in some professional areas, including accountancy and the law. You can be self-employed, but you will have to declare the name in which you were made bankrupt on your business correspondence and records so that people running credit checks on your business will be able to find out your full financial history. You may also be required to provide regular accounts to your trustee.

5: Protecting your family's finances

For many of us, the idea of controlling our financial affairs is intermingled with the notion of making money, of investing what we have to create an even bigger pot of gold. But it is equally important to protect what you already have against unexpected events. This chapter explains how to achieve this key goal by looking at:

- **Maternity and paternity benefits**

- **Children's benefits**

- **Insurance**

- **Money, love and splitting up**

- **Gay relationships and money**

Maternity and paternity benefits

Many expectant mothers are entitled to benefits such as Statutory Maternity Pay (SMP) or Maternity Allowance. This depends on your work status, how much you earn and how long you have worked for the same employer.

STATUTORY MATERNITY PAY

You can get SMP if you have been working for the same employer for at least 26 weeks by the time you are 15 weeks away from the date your baby is due. This means that you must have worked for the same employer throughout your pregnancy.

You should also earn at least as much as the lower earnings limit each week, which is the level of wages where National Insurance contributions (NICs) start. In the 2009–10 tax year, this was £95 a week.

SMP is paid by your employer and can be paid for up to 39 weeks. If you qualify for SMP, it is paid for the first six weeks at 90 per cent of your average gross weekly earnings, with no upper limit. For the remaining 33 weeks, at the lower end of either the standard rate of £123.06, or 90 per cent of your average gross weekly earnings.

Your employer will usually pay you in the same way and at the same time as your normal wages.

MATERNITY ALLOWANCE

If you are not entitled to maternity pay, you may be entitled to Maternity Allowance. This is a benefit for women who have been working but who do not meet the work and earnings conditions for SMP. You must have been working for at least 26 weeks in the 66 weeks before you are due to give birth, as long as you have been earning at least £30 a week on average. This can be from employed or self-employed work. Maternity Allowance does not depend on NICs.

The amount of Maternity Allowance you get is either 90 per cent of your average earnings or £123.06 a week, whichever is less. You may get an additional amount for your husband, civil partner, or someone else who looks after your children, if that person is on a very low income.

You can claim Maternity Allowance on form MA1, available from Jobcentre Plus in England, Wales and Scotland, or the Incapacity Benefits Branch in Northern Ireland (for details, see page 212) . Forms are also available from antenatal clinics and local benefits offices.

OTHER BENEFITS

If you haven't been working recently, making you ineligible for SMP or Maternity Allowance, you may be able to claim other benefits instead.

Employment and Support Allowance (ESA): Whether or not you are entitled to this depends on the stage of your pregnancy and whether there would be a risk to your health or your baby's health if you worked.

Income Support: If you are eligible, you can claim this once you are 29 weeks' pregnant, or earlier if you are incapable of work because of your pregnancy.

The rules about the benefits you can claim in pregnancy and early maternity are complicated. It therefore makes sense to speak to an experienced adviser, for example at a Citizens Advice Bureau near you.

MATERNITY GRANTS

Sure Start Maternity Grant: If you get benefits or Tax Credits because you are on a low income, you may be able to get this grant from the Social Fund. Worth £500, it can be spent on anything you wish and does not have to be repaid. There are, inevitably, conditions attached to how you can get a maternity grant. Basically, they are paid if you, or your partner, receive Income Support, income-based Jobseeker's Allowance or Pension Credit at the time of the claim.

If you get Child Tax Credit or Working Families Tax Credit, you may be able to get a maternity grant. Claim on form SF100 (Sure Start) from local benefit offices or antenatal clinics. You can claim from the 11th week before the baby is due and up to three months after the baby is born, or up to three months after the date of the adoption or parental order.

Health in Pregnancy Grant: This is a one-off grant of £190, available from HMRC. This grant is not means-tested and is payable as long as:

- You are 25 weeks pregnant or more
- You have been given health advice from a midwife or doctor.

Claim forms are available from your midwife or doctor, who fill in and sign part of it before handing it over to you. The fully completed form must be sent in to HMRC within 31 days of the doctor or midwife signing it.

PATERNITY BENEFITS

If you are a working father, or the partner of a woman having a child (including a same-sex partner), you may be able to get Statutory Paternity Pay (SPP) for two weeks during your paternity leave.

You can take statutory paternity leave if you are an employee with a contract of employment and have been with your employer for at least 26 weeks by the end of the 15th week before the start of the week when the baby's due. You must also be:

- The biological father of the child, or
- The mother's husband or partner (including same-sex relationships), or
- The child's adopter or the partner of the adopter, and
- Fully involved in the child's upbringing and be taking the time off to support the mother or care for the baby.

To qualify, your earnings must be at least the lower earnings limit for NICs. If your average weekly earnings are £95 or more before tax, SPP is paid for one or two consecutive weeks at £123.06 or 90 per cent of your average weekly earnings if this is less.

ADOPTION BENEFITS

If you meet certain qualifying criteria, you may be entitled to take 52 weeks' statutory adoption leave and receive Statutory Adoption Pay (SAP) for 39 weeks when you adopt a child. If you are adopting jointly, your partner may also be entitled to Statutory Paternity Leave (SPL), although it is possible to choose who will take SAL and who (regardless of gender) will take SPL. More details are available from www.direct.gov.uk.

Children's benefits

The two main benefits for children are Child Benefit and Child Tax Credit (CTC).

CHILD BENEFIT

Most people living in the UK can claim Child Benefit. It is a tax-free benefit that does not require NICs to be paid and is not means-tested.

It is payable to anyone responsible for a child aged under 16, or a young person aged under 20 if they are still in full-time education up to A level or equivalent, or on certain approved training courses.

Child Benefit is paid at a higher rate for your oldest child and at one rate for all your other children. In January 2009, the Child Benefit rate for the oldest child was £20 a week and £13.20 for other children.

You can claim Child Benefit by completing form CH2, available from HMRC enquiry centres or the Jobcentre Plus offices (see page 212 for details).

CHILD TAX CREDIT (CTC)

CTC is a payment for people with children, whether they are in or out of work. It is paid by HMRC if your income is low enough and you are responsible for at least one child.

The actual amount of CTC depends on your circumstances and your income. You can get it on quite high gross incomes, including incomes of over £50,000 a year. If you live with your partner, your incomes will be added together when your claim is assessed. Gross income means what your income is before tax and NICs are deducted. Some of your income – including Child Benefit, SMP and Maternity Allowance will be disregarded – when your eligibility for CTC is worked out.

top tip: savings do not affect your entitlement directly, but if you are getting interest of £300 or more from your savings, this is counted as income and will affect the amount of CTC due.

The actual amount you get is almost impossible to work out, but is made up of different elements.

Family element: This is payable to any family with responsibility for one or more children. The maximum payable in January 2009 under the family element is £545 a year. If you have a child in your family who is under one year of age, you get an extra amount of family element, sometimes called the baby element, worth up to £1,090 in 2009. This stops once the child reaches one year old.

Child element: This is payable for each child or young person in your family, regardless of the age of the child. There are extra amounts for children who are disabled and these are paid on top of the child element. If your child is registered blind or entitled to Disability Living Allowance, you will be able to get the disabled child element. If your child is severely disabled and entitled to the highest rate care component of Disability Living Allowance, you will get the severely disabled child entitlement as well. The maximum child element that can be paid is £2,235 a year, or up to £2,670 for a disabled child, depending on the disability.

To apply for CTC, contact the tax credit helpline at HMRC for an application pack or go to your local Jobcentre Plus (see page 212 for details). The application form for your first claim is form TC600. You apply for Working Tax Credit (WTC) on the same form (payable to someone working a minimum of 16 hours a week). You should answer all the questions on the application form in case you are able to get WTC as well.

The application form requires a lot of detailed information, including your income for the previous tax year. If you have problems filling in the form, check the notes that come with it, phone the Tax Credit helpline, or consult an experienced adviser, for example, at a Citizens Advice Bureau.

It is also important to keep as much evidence of your personal circumstances as you can. You should keep P60s (or P45s if you have left a job), statements about any benefits you receive and statements from your bank or building society about any savings. Documentation about your income or capital will help you to fill in the form.

Change of circumstances

Tax credits are awarded for a complete tax year, from 6 April to the following 5 April. If your circumstances change, tell HMRC as soon as possible. Otherwise you may be underpaid – or you may be overpaid, in which case your benefits can be clawed back the following year. You may be able to get some CTC for a period before you apply, if you met the conditions and could have claimed earlier.

OTHER FINANCIAL HELP

When you get CTC, you may be entitled to other financial help. If you pay rent, you may be able to get Housing Benefit. If you have to pay Council Tax, you may be able to get Council Tax Benefit. CTC is taken into account as income for both these benefits, which means that it affects the amount of Housing Benefit and Council Tax Benefit you can get.

Guardian's Allowance

If you look after a child who is not your own (biologically or by adoption), you may be entitled to Guardian's Allowance. This is a tax-free benefit payable by the Child Benefit Office (part of HMRC) and is worth £14.10 each week for each qualifying child. The form to claim with is BG1, available from HMRC and Jobcentre Plus (see page 212).

Disability Living Allowance

You can get Disability Living Allowance for a child who has care needs or mobility problems. Care needs include help with washing and dressing, and mobility problems means having difficulty walking at an age when most children would not need help. Children under 16 cannot claim Disability Living Allowance in their own right, so usually you will claim this for your child if you are his or her parent or guardian.

Help with childcare costs

CTC does not include any help with the costs of childcare. However, WTC does include some help towards childcare. If you are working and you are on a low income, you may be entitled to WTC.

If you are not getting WTC, there may be other help with childcare you can access. Lone parents on the New Deal for Lone Parents, may get help with childcare if they need to do a training course or look for work.

Insurance

Insurance can seem boring, but for many people, taking out the right kind of cover is an essential part of protecting themselves and their families against an untoward event.

LIFE INSURANCE

Unless you have no dependents – and therefore no one who needs looking after financially in the event of your death – the most important form of cover is generally considered to be life insurance.

How much life cover do you need? Many financial advisers use a simple formula where they multiply each family income-earner's salary by 20. This is based on the assumption that the lump sum available from the policy will deliver an income of about 5 per cent. Both partners in a relationship need to take out cover in relation to their own earnings.

A more sophisticated approach is to:

Add any immediate expenses after death, including funeral expenses and legal costs.
Deduct any other insurance already available through work.
Add the effect of a spouse's death on the remaining partner's income, especially where children are involved. There may be nanny's fees involved, for example.
Deduct additional investments, including any pension, set aside for this possibility.
Consider whether the mortgage will be paid off as a result of separate cover, perhaps through an endowment policy or similar.

For more information on how to calculate the amount of life insurance that you may need, go to: www.which.co.uk/reviews-ns/life-insurance/how-much-cover.

Types of cover

Next, you need to work out what kind of life insurance you need.

Whole-of-life: This is a policy common in the 1970s and 1980s and was still sold to people with complicated Inheritance Tax (IHT) planning needs. Essentially, with a whole-of-life policy, as long as the premiums are met, a payout will be made. The protection is not for a fixed period but it can last indefinitely, typically (though not always) subject to regular reviews, which generally take place every five or ten years.

Premiums are invested in the stock market, after taking out expenses and the provision of immediate cover. In the past, good stock market performance meant there was a chance that premiums would stay the same or, in some cases, even fall. Today, share price volatility can mean that premiums going forward are much higher at review times and often become prohibitive as people reach retirement age.

Term cover: This is by far the most common type of cover. It works by insuring your life for a set number of years for an agreed amount. If you die, the policy pays out. If you don't die, the policy lapses at the end of the term. Term cover policies are generally sold as 'level term', where both premiums and benefits payable remain the same throughout their lifetime. For policies linked to mortgages, it is possible to take out 'decreasing' cover. This is where benefits paid reduce over the course of the term. Although cheaper, many advisers prefer level term cover, as mortgages are not usually the only thing life insurance is taken out to protect.

Family income benefit (FIB): Some people prefer to ensure their families will receive an annual income over a set number of years. This is what FIB policies do: you decide on the income and how many years you want it to last, usually until children are grown up, then insure for that period of time. The policy will pay out on death.

If you die with ten years to go, it pays out ten years' income. If you die after five years, the policy pays over that remaining period of time, and so on. The advantage is that an FIB is cheaper than typical life insurance. Also, because an FIB provides a guaranteed income, it can offer a greater security than simple lump sums, which then need to be invested.

Writing a policy in trust

When you take out life insurance, you don't want payouts to fall foul of IHT. Moreover, you want the money to go to your dependents quickly, without having to settle the estate first.

Writing an insurance policy 'in trust' ensures that the policy pays out direct to your dependents, bypassing your estate altogether. Most insurance companies have standard forms for doing this and it usually costs nothing to write your policy in trust. Therefore, if your life insurer doesn't ask you first, make sure you get one of these forms, fill it in and send it back.

Joint life: Instead of you and your partner taking out separate insurance policies, you could take out a joint life policy. This has some variants:

'First death' covers both your lives and pays out once on the death of the first of you to die

'Last survivor' pays out once on the death of the second of you to die.

For protecting dependents, the 'first death' option is usually more appropriate.

A joint life policy is suitable if you both need to insure for the same amount, such as paying off a mortgage. But it is less suitable as a means of replacing lost income, since the income needs will vary depending on which of you has died. For that, it may make sense to insure separately.

Life-of-another: One spouse or civil partner may take out insurance against the life of the other. However, at the time the policy is taken out the insurer must have an 'insurable interest' in the life of the person covered. This means that one must stand to lose financially if the other were to die. Others may be permitted in discussion with the life company concerned.

If your relationship breaks down, your former spouse or partner retains the right to a payout in the event of your death. On the other hand, where a relationship has already broken down, a life-of-another policy that is taken out by one parent – with the children being identified as the beneficiaries – protects the family against the loss of maintenance payments.

PERMANENT HEALTH INSURANCE (PHI)

All of us worry about dreadful diseases like cancer. Yet we rarely think about how we would survive financially if something happened, but we carried on living for many years. Yet evidence suggests that a long-term inability to work is far more common than many people realise.

PHI, also known as income protection, pays out an income in the event of an illness that prevents you from working. It pays up to 60 per cent of your salary free of tax (or 75 per cent if it is an employer's policy – but you are taxed on the income) either until you are able to resume work again, or until the plan expires, typically at retirement age. Here are five rules to follow if you decide to take out PHI cover:

1 Before you buy, check whether you have some form of cover through your employer. If you haven't, find out what your employer's sick payment scheme offers as generally PHI policies are timed to kick in after a sickness scheme runs out.

You can then decide when you want your PHI to start. This can be at any time from four weeks to two years after you become ill, depending on the plan. Many employees tend to start payouts as soon as their company sickness benefits end. But the longer you hold out before you start taking payments, the lower the cost of monthly premiums.

2 Choose which type of cover you want. There are three types:
Guaranteed. Contributions remain level through the plan term. This is cheapest, but the benefits will be eroded by inflation.
Reviewable. Premiums are reviewed at stated intervals.
Age related. Premiums increase by a set amount each year.

3 Decide how much income you want to protect. The most common rule is that the income paid out by the policy, plus any other income from sources such as Statutory Sick Pay, state benefits and any other insurance, must not equal more than three quarters of your pre-tax earnings over the previous 12 months.

In the case of the self-employed, the insurer will usually calculate assumed annual income by taking an average of three years' worth of taxable earnings. However, the income you receive is free of tax, so you are not as badly off as you think. If your PHI is arranged by your employer under a group scheme, then benefits are taxable.

4 Decide whether you need 'waiver of premium'. This ensures your premiums continue to be paid while you remain unable to work. Waiver of premium is worthwhile if you are likely to be off work for a long time.

5 Choose whether you want an 'own occupation' or 'any occupation' clause. The former means the policy will pay out if you are unable to do your own job. The latter means it pays out if you cannot do any job. For example, the insurer might argue that a former steeplejack who is now in a wheelchair can still work in an office and cut benefits accordingly. Which? recommends you only choose a policy that pays out for 'own occupation' or an 'occupation for which suitable or trained'.

Things to watch out for

Medical evidence is always required and cover will be more expensive for those in poor health, while existing medical conditions may either be excluded, lead to you pay more or have cover declined.

Premiums are almost always higher for a woman than for a man of the same age and occupation: statistics show that women are more likely on average to suffer ill health during working ages than men.

Many policies are reviewable: if overall claims history (not your individual ones, but those of all policyholders), are greater than anticipated, premiums can rise across the board.

CRITICAL ILLNESS INSURANCE

If you are worried about the possibility of contracting cancer or suffering from a stroke or heart attack – illnesses that have the power to kill or leave you in pain and facing lingering disability – you may want critical illness insurance. Indeed, for many years, this type of cover was once called 'dread disease' insurance.

In most cases, people can survive these diseases for years after diagnosis, but going back to work and looking after your family financially is another matter. Critical illness insurance aims to remove this worry, by paying a tax-free lump sum on diagnosis of a specific

top tip: critical illness insurance is a 'luxury product' and should only be taken out if both income protection and life insurance are in place.

life-threatening medical condition or if the policyholder becomes disabled and is unable to work again. Unlike life assurance, which pays out a lump sum to dependents but only on a policyholder's death, critical illness insurance is paid on immediate diagnosis of an illness.

There some core diseases common to all policies: cancer, heart attacks, heart-by-pass surgery, kidney failure, major organ transplants, multiple sclerosis and strokes. Some policies contain a far longer list, including Alzheimer's, Aids or motor neurone disease. Total permanent disability – typically the result of an accident – is sometimes covered, and is worth having.

How critical illness insurance works

You pay monthly premiums for an agreed period of time. Should you be diagnosed as having one of the illnesses set out on your policy, the insurer will pay out an agreed lump sum, free of tax. Should your policy expire without you having contracted any of these illnesses, you receive nothing. When buying critical illness insurance, here are a few issues to consider:

1 How much cover you need. Most people tend to look for a lump sum large enough to pay off their mortgage, plus a bit over for any other immediate emergencies. If your mortgage is small, or if the cost of a policy puts you off, think about a lump sum you might need to give yourself the kind of treat you have always dreamed of. For example, a round-the-world cruise.

2 What you need cover for. There are many different policies, offering cover for a wide range of conditions. In practice, you will be torn between protecting yourself against everything and being more selective. For example, we have already mentioned Alzheimer's: but most people contract this illness after 55, so if you are 35 years old, why pay more to guard against it?

3 How long you need the policy for. Most people tend to have it either for the duration of their mortgages or until they retire.

4 Protection against inflation. You can have automatic updating of payouts – of course, you end up paying more for them.

5 Death within a few days of diagnosis. Most insurers won't pay out if you die between 14 and 28 days of diagnosis. The easy way round this is to have what is called 'accelerated life insurance' – that is, a combination of life and terminal illness cover. Payout happens on diagnosis of a dread disease or death, whichever comes first.

6 If your other benefits would be affected. Some state benefits – like the State Pension – are not means-tested, so you would still be able to claim despite a lump sum payout.

Things to watch out for

Many policies protect against 'total permanent disability' and being unable to work. Generally, look for a policy that has an 'own occupation' definition of work, as opposed to 'any occupation' (see page 84).

Some policies can be bought as standalone products, while others can be combined with life cover. The two together are often cheaper. Be aware, though, that if you do that, you won't get a second payout at death and you may find it virtually impossible to get any separate life cover going forward.

You can get deals that cover married couples on a 'first person to get ill, gets the payout' basis. These policies are cheaper than two separate ones and they do not usually affect the ability of the non-critically ill partner to get cover in future.

Some companies will follow the exclusions in their small print to the letter, so it is important to go to someone with a good claims history. Generally, these firms are known to most good IFAs.

Critical illness insurance pays good commission to those who sell it. Ask your adviser to pay you some of his commission. If he or she is not interested, others will be.

Some policies have reviewable premiums, which means you might end up paying a lot more after a number of years.

If you die shortly after the lump sum is paid out, any amount left is added to your estate and your heirs may be liable to IHT. Talk to a lawyer about how to reduce that danger.

PAYMENT PROTECTION INSURANCE (PPI)

This kind of cover meets loan payments on your behalf if you are unable to make them as a result of accident, sickness or unemployment. It can either be for a fixed period or, more often, it is indefinite: it ends when your loan does.

Single premium PPI

Until recently, most policies were sold on a single premium basis, meaning that a one-off premium would be added to a loan at the outset, although the borrower then repaid it by means of a regular monthly sum that was added to the sum borrowed.

Single premium cover is therefore enormously expensive. Research by the Citizens Advice Bureau found that the cost of single premium PPI could reach as much as 25 per cent of an unsecured loan – and 45 per cent for some types of HP agreements on car purchases. That didn't even cover the interest added to the cost of that policy as it was being paid off.

After years of complaints and a long investigation by the Office of Fair Trading, in January 2009 the Competition Commission announced a ban on the sale of PPI for seven days after a loan or another credit product, such as a credit card, is agreed. However, consumers can contact their loan providers after 24 hours to buy the cover.

The new measures, which come into effect in 2010, will also see a complete ban on single premium policies. The Competition Commission's ruling coincided with a parallel announcement by most major lenders, including Alliance & Leicester, Barclays, Co-operative Bank, Lloyds Banking Group and RBS/Natwest, that they would cease selling single premium PPI.

Regular premium PPI

With a regular premium policy, you pay for the cover you need on a month-by-month basis and can end payments at any time.

The problem is that the regular premium policies some lenders have replaced their old cover with are just as expensive. In June 2009, research by Which? found that taking out a £5,000 Alliance & Leicester

top tip: the lesson to learn is that if you feel you need payment protection cover, shop around for the best deal.

loan with regular premium PPI costs the same as it would have done with single premium PPI in November 2008.

Adding single premium PPI on to a £5,000 loan repaid over three years at 8.9 per cent APR from Alliance & Leicester added £1,016 to the cost of the loan in November 2008. Yet figures from the Financial Services Authority showed that the same loan from Alliance & Leicester at the same rate with a regular premium PPI in May 2009 costs the same amount of money.

In addition to its expense, Citizens Advice found that consumers found it much harder to claim on their PPI polices than on other insurance products. This particularly applies to self-employed and short-term contract workers. In the case of the self-employed, an insurer often only pays out if that person goes out of business, rather than simply being unable to get new work in. For this reason, many consumer experts, including Which?, recommend that this type of policy is not worth buying: the cover extends only to a single credit agreement, not the far wider range that most households tend to have in place.

Indeed, if you took out PPI with a loan or another credit arrangement, you may have grounds for compensation for mis-selling. If you feel this is the case, go to the Financial Ombudsman Bureau website (www.financial-ombudsman.org.uk), which gives details of how to complain on its home page.

MORTGAGE PAYMENT PROTECTION INSURANCE (MPPI)

This is a type of payment protection cover used to protect mortgage payments in the event of sickness accidents or unemployment. Having protection in the event of not being able to pay a mortgage is often seen as sensible.

An MPPI is available through mortgage lenders or from specialist insurers. Typically, a policy may cost £5–£6 for every £100 of monthly mortgage payments it protects against. So a £500 monthly mortgage could cost up to £30 a month to protect. However, specialist insurers can be significantly cheaper than lenders, so it pays to shop around.

Many MPPIs also cover against unemployment, although there can be rules that govern how long a policy must have been in force before you can claim. Also, you may face a long waiting period after you become unemployed until you can claim and they may only be made for a year or two. In most cases, this should be enough until you get back on your feet.

But should you take out mortgage protection? Before you do, work out whether you really need it.

You may well have some money saved up for a rainy day that could tide you over for a few months in the event of an emergency.

If you fell ill, your employer might have a good sickness scheme in place. Many will pay some or all of your wages for a minimum period if you are ill. At the very least, you are entitled to Statutory Sick Pay (SSP). From April 2009, this is paid at a fixed rate of £79.15 a week for a period of up to 28 weeks. This could help you meet your loan repayments.

If you are made redundant, you might have received a payout that could be used to make a few mortgage payments until you find work again.

You might be in the kind of job where finding work is not too difficult and therefore MPPI is not so necessary.

Check what help might be available from the State – see the information about Homeowners Mortgage Support on page 184.

Things to watch out for

Self-employed people and short-term contract workers sometimes find it hard to claim for unemployment.

You will not be able to claim for any time off work due to an illness or disability that existed before you took out the policy.

There is always a waiting period, usually ranging between 30 and 180 days before policies pay out when a claim is made.

The policy will usually pay out for up to 12 months only, although some insurers offer longer benefit periods.

The longer you can wait before you claim, the cheaper the cover. For example, if you are made redundant, you may be able to use some of that money towards your mortgage payments.

PRIVATE MEDICAL INSURANCE (PMI)

PMI is designed to cover the costs of private medical treatment for curable short-term illness or injury (acute conditions). PMI policies offer a range of benefits, usually divided into standard and comprehensive, and it is often possible to add certain elements to your standard cover on a 'modular basis'. The sort of things that might be covered by PMI include:

Accommodation and nursing in a private bed, in a hospital or registered nursing home while you receive treatment for illness or injury.

Home nursing benefits, payable when the services of a qualified nurse are required for full-time nursing at home.

Surgeons' and anesthetists' fees for an operation, including aftercare.

Courses of radiotherapy.

Specialists' fees for consultations, pathology and radiology investigations and physiotherapy, received on an in-patient or outpatient basis.

Fees charged by the hospital for the use of the operating theatre and for surgical dressings and drugs prescribed for use while an in-patient.

Cash benefit while treatment is being received free of charge under the NHS in an NHS hospital (either by choice or in an emergency). The amount may be fixed, or calculated as a percentage of the comparable private treatment.

Standard plans will not normally cover outpatient, routine maternity or dental costs. Comprehensive plans have higher limits and may cover outpatient care specialists, complementary medicine, dental treatment (or cash towards it), routine maternity care and personal accidents.

Exclusions

Generally, chronic long-term illnesses, for example emphysema, are excluded from cover. The other most common exclusions include: drug abuse, self-inflicted injuries, outpatient drugs and dressings, HIV/AIDS, infertility, normal pregnancy, cosmetic surgery, gender reassignment, sterilisation, kidney dialysis, mobility aids, experimental treatment, experimental drugs, organ transplant, war-related injuries (although some people may have this cover through their workplace), injuries arising from dangerous hobbies (often called 'hazardous pursuits').

Pre-existing conditions are generally excluded, other than with moratorium policies (see opposite). This is typically defined as a condition that has been diagnosed and required medical treatment in the past. Or it is one that you have sought medical advice for, or where symptoms have occurred in a period immediately prior to you applying for the plan. If the application form gives details of medical conditions that you have recently suffered from, sometimes going back as far as five years, an insurer will exclude those conditions from cover. Or the amount of cover you are offered may be reduced.

In addition, insurers may ask for a medical history questionnaire to be completed and signed. Or they may write to your GP or ask you to

Moratorium cover

This means you are not asked to give details of your medical history when you apply for cover. Instead, the insurance company does not cover any medical condition that existed in the last five years.

These conditions may automatically become eligible for cover, but only when you do not have symptoms, or receive treatment, medication, tests and advice from your GP or a specialist for that condition for a continuous period of at least two years after your policy has started. Of course, the moment you claim for any of these illnesses, it carries out checks then. So before taking out moratorium cover, always make sure the salesperson explains its implications and how his or her company applies it.

undergo medical tests. It is essential that you provide all the information required to avoid future questions or worse, rejection of claims.

How to cut PMI bills

The most obvious thing to look out for is to make sure that you are not covered by a workplace policy. If you are, you may also be offered a discount in respect of your family's cover. Otherwise, here are ways to cut the bill:

Pay an excess, where the first £200 or £500 of a hospital bill is met by you.

Receive treatment in a specified hospital, rather than one chosen by you.

Accept a slightly lower grade of hospital accommodation or in an NHS hospital.

Accept NHS treatment under the NHS if it is available within 6 to 12 weeks.

Some policies operate no-claims discounts; if you do not believe you are likely to claim often, look for an insurer offering this option. But if you do need to claim, don't hold back simply because you want to keep premiums low.

Consider 'self-insurance', another way of saying that you will pay for your own treatment.

If you have cover through your workplace and leave that employer, ask the insurer about continuing your cover at a preferential rate. Many will be willing to do this, especially if you have a good claims history, as they would rather keep you on the books.

Money, love and splitting up

When two people start to live together, they generally do so because they love each other. The issue of how to share their finances rarely enters into the equation. However, evidence suggests that money can cause major problems in many people's relationships.

AVOIDING DISAGREEMENTS

One recent survey found 40 per cent of the 145,000 or so divorces in the UK last year were actually about money, so a few ground rules agreed at the start can avoid painful disagreements months or years down the line. There are a few steps you should always follow:

Be completely honest with your partner at the outset: If you are going to live together, discuss how you each feel about spending money, obtaining credit, paying bills on time, being in debt and all the other financial activities that are likely to come up in your daily lives.

Make sure you agree in advance exactly how all the bills are going to be shared out between you: A joint account, into which you both pay an amount from your own personal accounts and from which household bills are paid, is a starting point. It may not always be the same amount, especially if one of you earns a lot more than the other. Or you may prefer to keep your financial independence and retain control of your earnings over and above any joint bills.

Do not agree to be the guarantor for any of each other's loans or credit agreements: You may end up being made responsible for them if the other person is unable to pay. In the early stages, if either of you wants to buy an expensive item, for example a car, make sure the ground rules (which should have been agreed already) cover what happens to it if anything should happen, including sickness, unemployment or a relationship breakdown.

If you decide to buy a house, an agreement over who pays and in whose name the property is placed becomes essential. This includes how much each of you will put in as a deposit, plus legal and other purchase costs and legal forms of home ownership (see page 93). Also, as with any rentals, how you will pay the bills, including the mortgage, insurance and utilities.

The important point for either person entering a relationship is to ensure that any financial contribution to a property is recognised by having their name on the title deeds and a declaration of trust to set out the financial contribution. They should contribute to the mortgage rather than pay the housekeeping.

Think about making a will: This is especially important if you are not married, as the UK's intestacy laws mean there is no provision for a surviving life partner. If there are no children, then the estate passes to the parents, siblings and other relatives in a specified order.

Gay couples who live together also have no special legal rights against each other unless they have registered their relationship as a civil partnership under the Civil Partnerships Act.

RELATIONSHIP BREAKDOWN

Amid the trauma – and, sometimes, the relief – at the ending of a relationship, sorting out the financial side of splitting up tends to come last on the list of priorities. Overleaf are some areas worth looking at.

top tip: the law varies depending if you are separating after being married or cohabiting, and with that comes different financial consequences.

Create a balance sheet

Although responsibility for who pays off debts or retains assets may have to be decided by a court, or through legal negotiation, drawing up a simple balance sheet is the first step. Both sides need to draw up details of what they own, what is owed and of all earnings. This should include every financial arrangement made as a couple, from bank accounts, not just joint ones, to hire-purchase agreements, loans and the mortgage.

Start the process

Contact all joint-name credit and store card issuers and stop the accounts. Close any joint bank accounts or at least notify the bank about the separation and reach an agreement with your former partner about access to that account. If you took out joint loans, you are liable for your partner's debts, so it is vital to discuss how these will be repaid.

The mortgage

Whether you are married or unmarried, it is vital to check out the title deeds on a joint property. If you are married and the property is not registered in your name, you must 'register a charge' on the property with the local Land Registry office to ensure that your spouse cannot sell the home or remortgage without your consent.

You will need to know the Land Registry title number of the property (available from your bank or building society if you have a mortgage) and complete an application form – your solicitor can do this for you.

For unmarried couples, if the property was bought in joint names, then regardless of sexual orientation, it is possible to apply to the court for an occupation order, allowing you to stay and live in the home.

If both parties are contributing unequally to payments on the property, then this may be reflected in them being designated tenants-in-common (see page 193) and holding unequal shareholdings, rather than the equal shareholdings of beneficial joint tenants.

Also, if you have a child from the relationship, the court has power under the Children Act 1989 to transfer ownership or allow one partner occupation of the home if it is in the interests of the child.

Even if the property is in the partner's name, an unmarried partner may be able to make a claim on the basis of financial contribution through an equitable interest claim in respect of contributions –

> **top tip:** it is now possible in some cases to take out a mortgage based on maintenance payments. It may make sense to contact a mortgage broker to discuss this further.

mortgage deposit, monthly repayments, bill payments or other – they have made towards the property.

Strangely, an unmarried woman has a better claim in the event of the death of the partner compared with splitting up, by claiming against the estate if financial provision is not made for her in the partner's will.

An endowment mortgage

Deciding what to do with an endowment mortgage after a divorce depends on what else is happening with the family finances, but financial experts usually advise that payments into the endowment itself are kept going. This is because surrendering, particularly in the first ten or 15 years after they are taken out, may well result in a payout that is less than existing contributions. Unless the endowment is surrendered on a pre-agreed early surrender date, it will not benefit from the terminal bonus – often a significant proportion of total returns.

The alternative is selling it through a company specialising in trading endowment policies. Note, however, that unit-linked policies, where growth is directly based on stock market returns, are not saleable. Also, not all policies are sought-after, especially those started only in the past ten years.

An additional factor to bear in mind is that someone in poor health may not be able to get separate life insurance. The life cover element of an endowment policy therefore becomes crucial.

Insurance

Where maintenance payments are concerned, many divorcing spouses assume that as long as these are agreed and payments are kept up, financial arrangements have been settled, even in the event of a former spouse's death. Not so. Even if life cover exists through work, an ex-husband may be able to change the named beneficiary or get a new job, where the beneficiary is not named. If the cover forms part of a related pensions package, it is vital to note this down when considering a division of joint assets.

But in any event, revising all insurance policy arrangements you have made for your partner on your death is important. If maintenance payments are involved in any settlement, it may be wise to take out a life insurance policy on an ex-spouse or civil partner's life. Naturally, the person paying the maintenance also pays the premiums on the insurance policy. This is even more vital where children are concerned.

The pension

Since December 2000, the law on dividing pensions has changed. On divorce, a spouse (or, in some cases, civil partner), may now be entitled to half the main breadwinner's pension. This applies to any tax-free lump sum as well. It does not apply to couples who are cohabiting.

The general idea is to prevent hardship for a wife who may have given up her own career to raise a family, keep house, and otherwise make a very material contribution to her husband's success. In a minority of cases, the reverse applies and it is the ex-husband who may have a claim on his former wife's pension.

Company pension schemes are usually valued at their transfer value – the amount of money that would be transferred if the holder moved it to another company scheme. Private personal pensions are taken at their fund value. But valuing a pension fund is one thing, working out how to distribute it is quite another. There are a number of options available to divorcing couples.

There are two processes:

One is known as 'offset', the other 'earmarking'.

Offset allows one partner to keep the pension and award the other partner a greater share of the family home, for example. This has to be agreed by the court.

The court can also earmark one partner's pension. This means that when the pension finally pays out, in 20 years or so, part of the pension is reserved for the other partner.

The problem with this system is that a former partner has to wait for the ex-spouse or civil partner to retire before getting any money. If he or she chooses to retire late, you have to wait longer. If the ex-spouse or civil partner dies before retirement, you can sometimes be left with nothing.

Since December 2002 there is a third option, called pension splitting, where divorce courts can order the immediate splitting or sharing of pension funds. This means that one spouse can lay immediate claim to a percentage of their partner's pension pot and move the money to another fund. They no longer have to wait for their partner to retire. There can be a cleaner break in the divorce and it allows each partner more direct control over their finances.

The will

Your will is one of the things you should review if you are splitting up. When a divorce goes through, your ex-spouse or civil partner will be treated as if he or she had died on the date of the divorce. Gifts to a former partner are cancelled, as are rights to be an executor of the will.

Also, couples in second marriages with children from a previous marriage or who have bought in assets to the second marriage are vulnerable – their assets may not be distributed in the way they hope for after death.

Surprisingly, if a person makes a will and then separates from their spouse, then the will is still valid and any part of it that relates to the soon-to-be ex-spouse is still valid until the moment of divorce – which can be a good argument for re-writing the will quickly.

Gay relationships and money

The financial needs of people who are gay and lesbian are broadly the same as anyone else's. But the way society responds to those needs is different to those of 'straight' people.

HEALTH AND LEGAL RIGHTS
The two key factors that influence financial issues for gays and lesbians are health and the law.

LIFE INSURANCE, INCOME PROTECTION AND CRITICAL ILLNESS
Despite evidence of growing survival rates for people with HIV/Aids, many insurance companies continue to load premiums charged for life assurance, critical illness and income protection.

Applicants for life cover are almost always asked if they are gay or lesbian, even if not in a relationship at that time. They then have to fill in a 'lifestyle' questionnaire, in which they are asked about the number of past sexual partners they have had.

Depending on that answer, they may be asked to take HIV tests. Even if negative, the premiums will often be considerably higher than those for straight people.

The Association of British Insurers, the industry's trade body, has urged its members to ensure that all applicants, straight or otherwise, be asked if they practise 'safe sexual behaviour' as a politically correct alternative to only asking gay men.

Meanwhile, there are many insurers who do not impose such tough conditions. Among gay-friendly companies are Norwich Union/Aviva, Scottish Widows and Friends Provident.

Although there is no theoretical reason why this should happen, some lesbian women in relationships – especially those who answer

| **top tip:** if you lie on your life insurance application form, in the event of you or your same-sex partner dying, particularly of an illness such as Aids, cover may be voided.

questions about their sexuality honestly – have also found their premiums are higher.

Income protection insurance: This covers a wide range of medical conditions – excluding Aids. And exactly the same issues of loading apply here as they do with critical illness and life insurance.

In the case of critical illness: Although some policies do offer cover for accidental HIV/Aids infection, it is almost solely in an occupational context, for example a doctor or a nurse who contracts the illness.

PENSIONS AND INHERITANCE

Under UK law, occupational pension schemes (see pages 145–52) are allowed to restrict the payment of dependents' benefits (such as death-in-service or dependents' pensions) to a surviving partner by only taking into account service from 5 December 2005 (or 6 April 1988 in respect of contracted-out rights) when calculating survivors' benefits for civil partners.

Pensions

The Government's Civil Partnership Act has brought radical changes to key financial issues, including rights on benefits, inheritance and tenancy.

The Bill says all pension rights are the same as those for married couples, going forward from the date of registration. Some schemes will recognise civil partners fully, others will not. Occupational public service schemes will do so retrospectively to 1988. The State Pension system also goes back to 1988, which means that all contracted-in company pensions will have to recognise Civil Partners' entitlement back to 1988 for the State Pension element of the overall pension.

However, private company final salary schemes may or may not recognise past service – this is at the discretion of the trustees and members should seek clarification as your partner could be left with no entitlement to your pension benefits on your death either pre- or post retirement if you are not registered civil partners. Even if you have completed an Expression of Wishes form (sometimes called Nomination of Beneficiary form), and stated that on your death your pension benefits should go to your partner, the pension provider may ignore your wishes, if your circumstances are unusual.

Inheritance tax (IHT)

If you or your partner dies and you are registered civil partners, IHT (see pages 201–6) is not payable. Similarly, if you gift your civil partner assets, such as company shares, there is no Capital Gains Tax (CGT) to pay, the same as for a married couple (see pages 194–8).

Equally, if you are in a same-sex partnership and have not registered under the Civil Partnership Act and you leave all your assets to the survivor, tax at 40 per cent will be charged on the value over £325,000, as of the 2009–10 tax year.

If you do not make a will, your assets will not automatically go to your partner. If you gift your partner assets, you may be liable to CGT, although civil partners and married couples would be exempt.

PARTNERS NOT IN A CIVIL RELATIONSHIP: WHAT YOU CAN DO

Make a will and keep it up to date: new partner, new will.

If you and your partner are joint tenants, owning a property without any form of separate share or distinction between each other, and one of you dies, the other will automatically inherit the deceased's share regardless of whether there is a will.

If you are tenants in common, where the co-owners are regarded in law as having separate and distinct shares, there is no automatic inheritance and you need a will. If a property is originally bought as a joint tenancy but the joint owners later realise that they would prefer to hold it as tenants in common, it is possible to make the switch.

Put all life insurance policies in trust, so they avoid IHT. This may also mean that if you or your partner die without the mortgage being paid off, the value of the estate is calculated after deducting the outstanding mortgage – which you then pay off with the life policy on which no IHT was paid. This has the effect of reducing your overall IHT bill.

Do the same with your occupational death-in-service benefits.

If your relationship is solid, consider equalising the estate by the richer partner passing assets over to the less well-off one. A lifetime gift can be made provided the donor lives for seven years after making it.

6: Building up your savings

To most people, the notion of saving money seems pretty straightforward. After all, if you want to tuck money away all you need to do, surely, is open a savings account and either place a lump sum or set aside a certain amount every month into it? The reality is that things rarely are that simple. This chapter tackles the different ways to build your savings by looking at:

- **Saving or investing?**

- **Your savings timeframe**

Saving or investing?

To most of us, there is little difference between saving and investing: both actions involve placing money away to meet a future need. However, experts do distinguish between the two. Saving involves using low-risk deposit accounts typically offered by banks, building societies and similar financial institutions. Investing is about placing money into share-based products such as unit trusts.

Other distinctions involve how long the money is set aside for, with savings being a short- or medium-term process and investment being more for the long term.

The two methods of building a nest egg are interlinked, however, with most people preferring to do both. For those who don't like taking excessive risks with their money, even a 20- or 30-year investment strategy may well involve the sole use of savings accounts.

In any event, a significant number of the points in this chapter that apply to savings also make sense for investors – and vice versa.

WHY SAVING MATTERS
Before you even consider saving, there are two key things to understand.

You are not just saving for a time far away in the future
For many people, saving money is all about retirement and when they get old. That is true to some extent: the time when people are most likely to need access to funds they have saved up is when their earning power is more limited, typically when they finally stop work.

But in most cases, you will need access to the money far sooner than that, typically within five to ten years. The starting point here involves understanding that the credit crunch of 2007 and 2008 changed the ground rules when it comes to obtaining credit. For the foreseeable future, if you really want something that costs thousands of pounds, at the very least you will need to find a far larger deposit for it – or even buy it outright with your own money.

Saving actually works

Many savers worry that the amount they can realistically set aside is so puny that it hardly seems worthwhile. In fact, what they save will gradually grow faster, as a result of compounded interest. This means that interest is added not just to any monthly amount you set aside but also to the interest already there.

Imagine you put £1,000 into a savings account and the interest on it is 5 per cent a year. After 12 months, your savings would be worth £1,050. After two years, that sum is now worth £1,102.50, because interest at 5 per cent was added not just to the original £1,000 but also the £50 interest accrued in the first year. And so on. After 30 years that initial £1,000 would be worth £4,321.94, with interest making up £3,291.40 of that amount, even though nothing is subsequently added to the original lump sum.

Of course, in reality things can be much more complicated. The chances are that you would be saving a monthly amount, not just a one-off lump sum; that monthly amount may go up or down, depending on how much you can afford at any one time; interest rates are likely to fluctuate, as they have done recently.

Most importantly, inflation eats away at the value of any savings: if annual inflation were 2 per cent throughout the previous example's 30-year timeframe, then the true value of that lump sum would be around £2,510 at today's prices. That may not seem like much, but it still means your savings pot has more than doubled in that time.

TEN KEY SAVINGS RULES

Assuming you accept there is a need to save, here are ten vital rules you should always follow when saving money.

1 Don't try to save if you have massive debts. Any interest you will earn is highly unlikely to be higher than what you owe on, say, a credit card charging a typical rate of interest of at least 15.9 per cent APR, a bank overdraft and even many loans (apart from a Student Loan). So it makes sense to pay off your high-interest debts first.

2 Set yourself some goals. Decide what you are saving for: any savings will almost certainly have several aims at once – some short-term goals (for example, a holiday or a car next year); a medium-term one (a deposit on a home in ten years' time); a long-term one (retirement) (see also pages 10–12).

3 Make your first goal an emergency fund. You never know when disaster might strike: a sudden illness or an accident, being made redundant, a central heating boiler, your car or a computer packing up just when you need it most. Most experts suggest you should have at least two or three months' worth of after-tax income set aside to meet any emergencies if they arise. In practice, this is not always possible. But even a smaller fund of a few hundred or £1,000 will help enormously. If you can't manage this, be prepared to use your other short-term funds as and when necessary.

4 Understand your attitude towards risk. There is no point in investing in shares if you are likely to constantly worry that their price will tumble in the short and medium term. Share prices are volatile and can both rise and fall sharply for years at a time – although they do historically deliver better returns than standard saving accounts over longer time periods of 15 years or more.

5 Spread your savings and investments. This may seem obvious, but many people tend to chase after the best rate and think nothing of placing all their money in a single account, regardless of the potential consequences. The experience of almost 200,000 savers who almost lost all their money in Icelandic bank accounts in 2008 because they were not protected by Icelandic depositors' protection schemes, should serve as a warning (see pages 110–12).

Similarly, many investors think purely in terms of buying individual shares or even one or two funds. The problem with this approach is that if that share or fund nosedives, they risk losing a lot of money. The key to reducing volatility (sharp up and down movements) and not losing money is to diversify your investments as much as possible.

6 Get advice. There are very few people competent enough to handle their own saving and investment strategy from beginning to end. This means everyone needs at least one or two people to help, possibly both of them: an independent financial adviser (IFA) (see pages 23–30) and a fund manager, who is a specialist when it comes to buying equities. He or she will invest clients' money into a range of shares or similar.

7 Know that charges and fees matter. Most people who invest tend to think that performance is the key to the returns they are likely to receive. They are right, of course. But there is another factor to consider: savings and investment charges. This is the amount you pay to have your money looked after.

For savings accounts, there are no explicit charges – but you may face penalties for early withdrawals of cash, or be offered accounts with tiered rates of interest, or where a bonus is paid if you do not touch your money. Though not charges, strictly speaking, they do impact on your total returns.

For investments, any charges are more explicit: you are told what it will be before you buy and it usually reflects itself as an initial investment fee, which can be up to 5 per cent of the funds you invest, as well as an annual charge of around 1.5 per cent or more of the funds under management. Some funds charge less, others more.

Yet research repeatedly shows that, with few exceptions, most funds tend to deliver roughly similar performance over long stretches of time, usually within a relatively minor percentage range of each other. This means charges can have a disproportionate impact on the overall returns you will receive. For example, a 2 per cent annual charge over 25 years means your total fund will be worth 25 per cent less than one charging 1 per cent and delivering the same performance.

This becomes all the more important if you bear in mind that total charges do not simply include the management fee. What is even more important is a fund's total expense ratio (TER), which includes not only the manager's annual charge, but also costs for other services paid for by the fund, such as the fees paid to the trustee (or depositary), custodian, auditors and registrar, as well as any marketing costs. These typically add another 0.5 per cent to a fund's annual costs, but in some cases have been known to double the management fee itself. All funds are now required to tell you their TER in the product literature you are given, so make sure you check yours.

8 Never invest primarily for tax purposes alone. Tax can take a large chunk out of your savings, which is why it generally makes sense to pay as little of it as possible.

For those who receive the right tax advice, this is not impossible: over the years, successive governments have launched various types of savings schemes, each with different tax advantages (or disadvantages). They sometimes scrap earlier schemes but often don't, so offering a greater choice of tax-saving options. Occasionally, tax advisers also discover various 'wrinkles' in the system and are able to advise people about which scheme is better than another for tax purposes.

9 If it sounds too good to be true, it almost always is. This may sound like an obvious truism, but it is quite amazing how many people get caught . In fact, according to the Government's own figures, up to 28 million people are targeted each year and an estimated £1bn is lost to fraudsters.

Many of these scams come from so-called 'boiler room' operations using 'pump-and-dump' sales tactics that promise better-than-average returns. If such a strategy were successful, its merits would be widely discussed in the media and on reputable investment chatrooms. Lots of people would be urged to invest their money in such shares or schemes. The fact that this isn't happening should tell you something: the reality is there are very few best-kept secrets to investing, or unique strategies that someone hasn't tried before.

The FSA keeps an up-to-date record of all firms authorised to give advice or to do investment business in the UK. Indeed, firms themselves are required to state whether they are regulated and in relation to what activity. If in doubt, ask to see the firm's literature and look for details of FSA regulation – and then check out a firm's credentials with the FSA.

10 Keep an eye on your savings and investments. Just because your savings or investment decision may have been sound at the time it was made does not necessarily mean it is valid for all time. This means that if you opened a savings account, check it every six months to a year to make sure the rate you are being paid is among the best. If you are investing in shares or in a fund that itself invests in shares, talk to your adviser at least once a year to make sure the factors that determined your original decision still hold true today.

Your savings timeframe

Building on the goal-setting exercise in Chapter 1, a key determinant for meeting your goal(s) is likely to be how long you are saving for and what product you choose to save in. Here are some ideas of what you should do if you are saving for the immediate, short, medium and long term – and why.

IMMEDIATE SAVINGS

You should be looking at saving between one and three months' net earnings, so consider saving an emergency fund in a:

High interest savings account. Look for one with fast or even immediate access to your cash. You want to be able to transfer money within three to five working days, the amount of time it takes to book a heating engineer to fit a new boiler, for instance.

Flexible or offset mortgage. Using the scope to draw back down overpayments. But make sure you know how long it might take to gain access to this money.

SHORT-TERM SAVINGS

If you are planning on saving over two to five years, you will have a few more options.

High interest savings account: Again this is the place to put your money if you are certain that you do not intend to touch it for one or more years – and have a separate emergency fund in place.

This may not always sit well with investors, particularly if share prices are rocketing, but shares are just too volatile to dabble with over short periods. Although returns can sometimes be significant – in the four-year period between April 2003 and April 2007, the FTSE 100 index of leading UK shares rose about 60 per cent – prices can also fall sharply, as many people experienced between 2007 and 2009.

Looking at the same index, in mid-June 2009 the FTSE 100 stood 46 per cent down on the level it achieved in the same month ten years before. It was also down slightly on the same point five years ago, in June 2000. This is not the full story: many quoted company shares pay dividends twice a year to their owners and reinvested dividends often form the largest part of investors' overall growth. But dividend yield can also rise and fall, along with a company's share price.

Fixed-rate bonds: If you already have a sizeable lump sum to invest, one option could be a fixed-term bond, effectively a fixed term, fixed rate deposit account. These generally allow you to make a single payment then leave the account to let your money grow with interest.

When the term ends you are given your money back, plus the added interest. Note that some fixed-term accounts will not allow you to withdraw your money until the term ends. Others may levy a charge, or lower the interest rates for the month that the withdrawal was made.

National Savings & Investments (NS&I): Another safe place for your money is NS&I, the Government-backed savings institution. The fact that it is linked to the Government means your money is reckoned to be ultra-secure, or at least as safe as it can be in the current climate.

NS&I offers a range of tax-free saving schemes, often for fixed periods of up to five years. Some of them guarantee to pay above existing inflation rates, although that figure tends to be adjusted up or down, depending on what happens to retail prices.

top tip: overall, the rates paid by NS&I are not as high as elsewhere in the private sector, but many people are prepared to trade higher returns for greater safety.

Cash ISA: If you are planning to save money in the short to medium term you may want to think about putting your cash into a cash ISA. For more information about ISAs, see opposite and pages 131–2.

Bonuses

When looking for a savings account, watch out for those where the seemingly high rate of interest is padded out by means of bonuses, or where there are excessive interest penalties for cash withdrawals.

Bonuses are used to make any interest payable look great: you might be offered 5 per cent, of which 3.5 per cent is the basic rate, plus an extra 1.5 per cent if you leave the money untouched for at least 12 months. In reality, many people find they need some of their savings back from time to time, which makes the real rate of interest much less interesting.

MEDIUM-TERM SAVINGS

If you are looking at a five to ten-year timeframe, you are still probably better off sticking with savings accounts as share volatility even over a relatively long period of ten years could affect the value of your savings.

So, much the same rules apply as with shorter-term investments, but perhaps with a slightly greater emphasis on the tax-free aspect. Although reducing the tax you pay is important, it becomes much more so over longer periods. If you are saving regularly and are paying basic rate tax on your income, you will also be liable to pay 20 per cent tax on any money in your savings account. In fact, your bank will already be deducting it for you and paying interest on your money net of tax.

Over two or three years, that may not matter so much. For example, say you have saved £1,000 in that time, earning 5 per cent annual interest. That 20 per cent tax deduction will reduce the amount of interest you receive by £10 over one year. But multiply those savings over ten years – and the amount you saved becomes a less modest £10,000, on which 5 per cent interest is accruing at a rate of £500 a year, and HMRC is now taking at least £100 a year – more, if you take into account the effect of compound interest referred to earlier. Sheltering your savings into an ISA therefore makes even more sense.

Stocks and shares ISA: From April 2010, you can hold up to £10,200 per year in an ISA, of which up to £5,100 of that allowance can be saved in cash with one provider. The remainder can be invested in stocks and shares with the same or a different provider, or the entire amount can be invested in stocks and shares. So once your timeframe begins to move outwards, think about using the second element of your ISA allowance for shares. The same restrictions apply as for a cash ISA (see pages 131–2).

LONG-TERM SAVINGS

Because you are considering tying up your money for ten years or longer, this is where potentially you have the widest range of options.

High interest savings accounts: For many people who are not keen on accepting any form of risk, high interest savings accounts will once again seem the safest option. As with short- and medium-term savings, you may want to place some of your money in fixed-rate accounts. Even so, there are two things to bear in mind:

Inflation can significantly affect the real returns from a savings account. If annual interest paid is 3 per cent but inflation averages 2.5 per cent, the real rate of growth is just 0.5 per cent a year.

Equity-based investments: Almost anyone thinking of saving for the long term should, however, consider investing in some form of share-based investment, which is what the next chapter is all about.

SAVINGS AND INVESTMENT PROTECTION

The financial crisis of 2007 and 2008 has thrown the issue of how well protected savers' funds are in the event of a bank collapse. The 'fund of last resort', which will pay out in the event of a financial institution going bust, is called the Financial Services Compensation Scheme (FSCS).

The FSCS, which is funded by a levy of all other financial services providers, steps in when it consider that business is unable to operate any longer. The rules it operates under are set by the Treasury and vary, depending on the type of business carried out by the firm in default.

Protection for savers

Under the terms of the FSCS, savings held with an FSA-registered provider are protected up to £50,000. Couples generally get the same level of protection. So, for example, if you have £100,000 in a joint account with your spouse, you get £50,000-worth of protection each. There are, however, some complications with the compensation system, outlined on the opposite page.

If you had £70,000 in a joint account and £30,000 in a sole account, the joint account would be split both ways. This means holders of money in the joint account would receive £35,000 each – while the owner of the sole account would only get £15,000, taking them up to the full £50,000 he is entitled to.

The £50,000 maximum (or double for couples) only applies to accounts at a single institution. So, for example, if you have money in both a Halifax account and an Intelligent Finance one, you would receive a maximum of £50,000 at present as they are all part of the same group operating under one licence. Where a joint bank operates separate banking entities, like Royal Bank of Scotland (RBS) and NatWest, the amount of compensation is £50,000 each for RBS and NatWest. Similarly, because Halifax and Lloyds TSB operate under different banking licences, despite HBOS having been taken over by Lloyds in 2009, savers with two separate accounts in each of the two banks would be entitled to receive up to £50,000 protection from each bank. Note that for offshore accounts, savers are not protected by the FSCS.

Case study

James is 27 years old and earns about £1,700 net per month after pension contributions. He shares rented accommodation, for which he pays £650 a month, including Council Tax and most bills. He drives a 1999-registered 1.25l Ford Fiesta, has savings of £850 and would like to move into new accommodation at £750 a month, but needs to find two months' deposit.

Goals
- A deposit for a new flat: £1,500 needed.
- To buy a better and more reliable car: £3,500 needed.
- Build up a big savings pot to finance a house purchase in ten years' time: £15,000.

Plan
- Negotiate deposit down to six weeks: £1,050. Give notice to existing landlord and top up existing savings with returned deposit to finance move into new accommodation.
- Take out a three-year loan for a car, paying £100 a month, and sell existing car for £500.
- Set up a cash ISA account and pay in £150 a month, more if possible. Assuming annual growth of 4 per cent, James' savings will grow to £22,000 over ten years.

Income Tax on savings and investments

You pay Income Tax on the income you get from your savings and investments. This includes bank and building society interest, dividends from shares and rents from any investment properties you own. Bank and building society interest and dividends are usually taxed at source, which means tax is deducted before the interest is paid to you.

The way tax is levied on savings is different to what you pay on your work-related income because although the Government scrapped the 10p starting tax rate for earned income, it has not done so for other income.

- The first £2,440 of savings income is taxed at 10 per cent, although in practice any tax payable is almost certain to be above this limit, as the interest is added to your other income.
- Savings income that rises above £2,440 but under £37,400 is taxable at 20 per cent.
- Earnings above that level are taxed at 40 per cent.

If you are a non-taxpayer you may be able to claim some tax back by asking your savings institution for form R85 (or go to www.hmrc.gov.uk/forms/r85.pdf). If you are a higher-rate taxpayer you will have more tax to pay.

The rules also mean that if you are married and open a joint account with your spouse, each of you will pay tax at your higher rate. If you want to reduce the level of tax payable on a joint account, it makes more sense for the lower or non-tax-paying spouse to have the account in his or her name. Alternatively, open an Individual Savings Account (ISA) (see pages 131–2).

GOVERNMENT GATEWAY

For millions of people, saving can be especially difficult, especially if they are on low incomes or in receipt of benefits. However, from 2010, there will be a new government-backed saving scheme called Saving Gateway, aimed at people of working age on lower incomes. The aim is to help kick-start a saving habit and follows trials in six parts of the UK.

Under the proposed rules, the Government will contribute 50p for each £1 saved into Saving Gateway accounts. You qualify for an account if you get certain benefits, which include: Income Support, Jobseeker's Allowance, Incapacity Benefit, Employment Support Allowance and Tax Credits, for those with incomes below £15,575.

The details were still not fleshed out at the time of writing and more information about Saving Gateway will be made available nearer to the launch in 2010. Those who qualify will be sent an information booklet.

7: Investments

Anyone with a long-term financial goal will inevitably find themselves having to consider an investment strategy at some stage in their planning. Nor is that so surprising: while savings accounts may pay a reasonable rate of interest, and your money is comparatively safe, anyone who wants better returns on their original capital – certainly growth that can outstrip inflation in the long term – needs to consider some form of equity investment. In this chapter, you will learn about:

- **Shares and the stock market**

- **How to invest in the stock market**

- **Investing free of tax**

Shares and the stock market

Unfortunately, investing in shares can sometimes leave people worse off if their value falls. So are there any rules for successful investment that will help you avoid any of those heavy losses in the stock market? This chapter looks at some investment strategies and how they can be used. It also looks at various financial products and explains how they work. However, there is no foolproof way of making money. Nor does this chapter claim to offer you one.

Ultimately, what determines an investor's overall returns is the stock market, which has been described in the past as, in essence, 'the sum total of mass fear and greed operating through electronic exchanges'. Even the most successful investors may lose a portion of their invested capital at some stage. If they are very good, they will make some or all of it back and even come out ahead, perhaps. But that can take years – and a positive economic tailwind.

HOW THE STOCK MARKET WORKS
Whenever long-term savers are trying to decide how to obtain the best returns for their money, they are invariably advised to invest in shares. The reason for this advice is that shares offer the potential for greater growth than, say, a savings account. To understand why, it is necessary to look both at shares and at stock markets.

A stock market is a platform for trading shares in publicly listed companies. Essentially, it acts as an exchange, where buyers and sellers of company shares – both private and institutional – interact with each other. Prices are set on the basis of supply and demand. Shares themselves are portions, or holdings, in an individual company listed on a stock market.

From the investors' perspective, owning shares in a company offers two sets of opportunities. If the company is successful and its profits grow, its shares will be in greater demand. This means they will rise in value and if an investor sells them, he or she will be able to obtain a higher price than was originally paid for them.

In addition, shareholders sometimes receive a proportion of any annual profits that are not reinvested in the company. This is known as a 'dividend' and is usually paid twice a year. The importance of dividend yields will be explained later in this chapter.

In theory, share prices can rise or fall on the basis two factors: the health of the company and that of the wider economy, which can, in turn, affect what happens to the business. In many cases, what drives the value of a share up or down is not always rigorous research into the underlying business. Market sentiment as to whether a particular company is a worthwhile investment or otherwise also plays an important role.

WHAT GOES UP CAN COME DOWN

Investing in shares can deliver significant growth. It offers the opportunity for people to reach their given goal much faster than they would otherwise be able to achieve if they simply left their money in a high interest savings account. But there are several key factors to consider as well.

Volatility

For many, the experience of 2007 and 2008, when share prices around the world fell by 40 per cent or more, can seem frightening. Indeed, one of the key aspects of equity investment is its potential volatility. Had you invested a lump sum in a fund tracking the top 100 UK companies' shares in June 1999, you would have ended up losing a significant amount of money ten years later.

But in investment, as with everything else, statistics don't always tell the full story. Every year, Barclays Bank publishes a document called the Equity-Gilt Study, an annual look at the relative performance of different assets people might hold as investments.

According to the Barclays Equity-Gilt study, there is a 99 per cent probability of equities outperforming cash savings over a period as short as 18 years. In fact, equities outperformed cash in 75 per cent of consecutive five-year periods and 93 per cent of ten-year periods too.

Risk

The statistics work both ways, of course. For example, if shares outperformed cash three quarters of the time over consecutive five-year periods, investors in shares lost money 25 per cent of all other five-year periods.

Also, the Equity-Gilt Study does not say by how much shares did beat cash deposits in those five-year periods. This raises another question: is the risk involved worth the return? If, hypothetically, you might only get an extra 2 per cent a year from investing in shares compared to a savings account, but risk losing 20 per cent of your money, is that an acceptable risk?

Over five years, possibly not. But over 40 years it could well be: that extra 2 per cent a year, spread over a much longer period, could be worth an extra 80 per cent in the total value of your funds. If that were your retirement income, it might make the difference between £10,000 a year and £18,000.

There are ways of reducing volatility and risk (see pages 126–7), but it is vital for anyone considering a share-based asset to understand that while investing in shares offers the potential for growth, it is also possible to lose money by investing in the stock market.

Moreover, stock markets never move in a straight line. If prices do rise over longer timeframes, they are also likely to fall: this means that any investment decision you make should be for at least 10–15 years, preferably much longer.

How to invest in the stock market

If you are looking to invest money, you will have many choices. The two most common ones are buying individual shares, usually from a stockbroker, or going for a collective investment, typically a fund such as a unit or investment trust.

INDIVIDUAL COMPANY SHARES

This involves an investor researching and buying (or selling) shares in a company. Unless they have a very good tip that an individual company share is likely to do extremely well, the general approach of sophisticated investors is to create a portfolio of shares with 10 to 50 or more individual holdings. This allows the investor the opportunity to diversify his or her assets, an important strategy that helps reduce overall risk and volatility.

Using a stockbroker

Buying shares involves using a stockbroker's services. There are several types:

Full advisory service: This is where the broker looks at your circumstances and devises a strategy to suit your needs. Your portfolio is monitored on a regular basis and your broker contacts you with suggestions of shares to buy or sell. However, you still have the final say. This level of service is likely to be expensive, costing at least £1,000 a year, often far more. It is mostly worth considering only if you have assets significantly greater than £100,000.

Discretionary service: Here a broker may buy and sell shares on your behalf without asking for your approval first. This is also a highly tailored service and can also be very expensive.

Execution-only service: This means that the broker will simply take your order and execute it for you. These brokers cannot provide any advice on your decisions, but many offer all kinds of research and online tools for everyone from the novice to the expert.

What you should look for in a broker

Quality of information, in the form of services that can help with your trading, such as price improvers, which scan the market to get the best possible price for your stock.

Speed of execution; telephone and internet services may give you access to instant dealing, while postal dealing takes a couple of days.

Markets available as there is a huge range of investment products on the market (see pages 124–6), many of which are now available through brokers.

Cost, which is reflected either as commission (all brokers charge dealing commission on stock purchases and sales) or a flat fee regardless of the size of the trade. Expect to pay at least £7 through the cheapest broker and £10–12.50 through a broker with a wider range of services. Other fees can include registration, custody and transfer out fees if you move to a different broker, plus charges for issuing stock certificates. You will also be charged a £1 fee on all transactions over £10,000 and Stamp Duty at 0.5 per cent of the value of the share purchases (1 per cent for Irish stocks).

Certificates or paperless shares. Most brokers now hold shares for clients in paperless form. This form of ownership – also known as a nominee account – dispenses with cumbersome certificates and allows deals to be paid for within three days instead of ten days.

COLLECTIVE INVESTMENTS

For most people, who don't have very large sums at their disposal or the time to research the shares they want to buy, the alternative option is that of collective investment schemes, also known as mutual funds. Here, the decision on which shares or other assets to buy are made by a fund manager, who uses money placed at his or her disposal by hundreds, even thousands, of investors to create a diversified portfolio on their behalf.

Fund sizes range between a few million pounds to several billion pounds. A typical fund will be invested in anything between 20 and 100 different company shares, according to a mandate that sets the guidelines for managers about how they should invest the money they have been entrusted with.

In turn, because the mandate is formally set out, investors know that the fund they are entrusting with their money has a precise investment area it deals in, for example biotechnology, bank shares, commodities or the Far East. That said, managers can change their funds' mandate if they believe it does not serve their interests anymore.

An investment fund allows you to capitalise on the skills of a manager as well the research expertise that he or she brings to bear to the task. Good managers have access to material about hundreds of companies and have the experience to trade day in and out, selling or buying as appropriate. They, or analysts working for them, visit these businesses regularly and discuss prospects with company executives.

Because they are looking after tens, sometimes many hundreds of millions of pounds, they can diversify their portfolios, reducing volatility and risk. For investors who may not have very large lump sums, they often offer a regular saving option, where you can place a few hundred pounds, sometimes as little as £25 a month, into the fund.

That said, there are issues that investors need to be aware of when placing money in a mutual fund:

Charges. Funds typically charge up to 5 per cent for each amount contribution, plus a further 1–1.5 per cent in annual management charges. There are further fees on top.

Investment styles. There are times when an investment style considered suitable in, say, a market upturn, is not suited to a different climate (see pages 126–7).

Fund manager departures. On average, a fund manager changes jobs every four years. This means that the fund you placed your money in last year, largely on the strength of an individual manager, may be run by a different individual using different investment criteria. That said, many funds operate on the basis of teams, of whom the manager is one member, albeit a senior one.

Types of funds

The choice is vast: there are more than 2,000 funds on the market, covering every possible sector, of which the two most common types are unit trusts and investment trusts followed by open-ended investment companies (OEICs) and investment bonds (see overleaf).

Unit trusts: This type of fund was first created in the early 1930s. Its aim was to offer a simple way for investors to hold a portfolio of shares whose overall price directly reflected the underlying assets owned by the fund itself. A unit trust is divided into units whose price is based on the fund's total net asset value (NAV). For example, a unit trust fund may invest £1 million into each of 20 different companies and gives its investors units in the trust, each worth £1. That means there are 20 million units in existence.

Crucially, the number of units in a unit trust is unlimited (it is 'open-ended'). So, when you invest in a unit trust, new units are created and allocated to you, based on the price in force at the time and how much money you are investing. The additional money can then be used to buy shares in more companies.

If the share price of the companies the manager has bought with your money (and everyone else's) goes up, so does your unit price – or vice versa. When you dispose of all or part of your investment, the units you have bought are cancelled and the money you receive is based on their price at the time of sale.

The structure of unit trusts means there is no underlying supply and demand issue related to the units. In turn, their value directly represents that of the assets the fund is invested in.

A unit trust's annual charges usually involve an investment fee of between 1 and 2 per cent, plus other services paid for by the fund (the total expense ratio (TER) (see page 105), which generally adds 0.5 per cent to a fund's total annual costs.

top tip: the initial charge levied on a unit trust is reflected in a 'bid' and an 'offer' price. This is the price at which a unit is sold ('bid') and a separate price at which it is bought ('offer'). The difference between the two can be up to 5 per cent.

Investment trusts: Investment trusts are 'closed-end' funds, set up as public limited companies and therefore quoted on the stock market. This means that there are a finite number of shares available for investors to buy.

Although the fund manager is buying shares in companies on behalf of the investment trust, investors are buying shares in the trust itself. In effect, not only can the value of the shares held by the trust go up and down, so do shares in the investment trust.

This can sometimes lead to a seemingly contradictory situation where the value of a trust's assets goes up but the trust's own share price falls. This is known as a discount to net asset value (NAV).

In and of itself, a gap between the share price of an investment trust and the assets it holds is not necessarily a problem. The potential problem is when the value of the underlying assets fall and the share price of the investment trust falls even further. In such cases, investors are caught by a double whammy.

Investment trusts are also allowed to borrow money, just like any other publicly quoted companies. This means they can borrow to invest, thereby offering the potential for greater gains if the investment goes well. But if the manager makes the wrong decisions, you risk losing even more.

Your attitude to risk

Every investment carries with it the risk that you may not get back some or all the capital. It is also generally the case that the highest returns involve the greatest risk to capital. Therefore, you need to decide how much risk you are prepared to accept to achieve a given goal. For some investors, risking more than 30 per cent of their capital each year in order to achieve annual returns in excess of 10 per cent is acceptable. Others may not see it that way.

If you are prepared to accept higher risk, your portfolio will reflect this fact. It may be skewed more towards potential high-growth investments, perhaps focusing on overseas markets where opportunities are greatest, or cutting-edge technology funds. Or if you are a low-risk investor, bond-based and other higher income-yielding funds will be preferable.

If you are a lower-risk investor, but you have a goal that will take a significant sum of money, then the only option to achieve that target is either to save more money or to do so for longer, or both.

Investment trusts are usually cheaper to buy than unit trusts. There are two charges: an initial charge (or entry charge) of between 0 and 4 per cent (many have no initial charge at all) and ongoing annual charges, which can be as low as 0.5 per cent. If you buy an investment trust's shares direct on the stock market, you don't have to pay the initial charge, though you will incur dealing charges and Stamp Duty.

Open-ended investment company (OEIC): This type of investment is very similar to a unit trust except that an OEIC is legally constituted as a limited company.

Most OEICS operate as umbrella funds, which means the OEIC can set up sub-funds with different investment aims. For example, a sub-fund may specialise in the shares of small companies or in a particular country such as the USA. Each sub-fund can also have different charges and minimum and maximum investments. Unit trusts are allowed to do this too, but few do.

For investors, this structure has some advantages: it means you can invest for income and growth in the same umbrella fund, moving your money from one sub-fund to another as your investment priorities or circumstances change. Some OEIC providers allow you to do this without charge.

The other key difference is that whereas a unit trust has two prices (bid and offer), most OEICS only have one unit price and the initial charge is added as an extra. It is this latter feature that has persuaded many unit trust managers to change the legal structure of their funds to an OEIC: doing so allows them to market their funds more effectively across the rest of Europe, where single pricing is far more common than the UK-style bid and offer structure.

Investment bonds: When you buy a bond you are allocated a certain number of units in the funds of your choice. Each fund holds a portfolio of investments, such as shares or bonds, and the price of your units – in other words the value of your capital – will normally rise and fall in line with the value of these investments.

Where investment bonds differ from unit trusts is in the way they are subject to tax. Technically, they are single premium life insurance

Top-slicing

When bonds are finally cashed in, any gains are taxed by means of the top-slicing rule, which favours higher-rate taxpayers who expect to move on to a lower tax band at retirement. This is because any liabilities are based on a taxpayer's income at the time.

Tax is calculated on the total profit the bond has made, divided by the number of years it has been held to calculate the annualised profit. So if you bought a £50,000 bond, which you held for ten years and it is now worth £80,000, this is the equivalent of annual gains of £3,000 a year.

If the combination of the annualised profit and your other income does not take you into the 40 per cent tax bracket, there is no more tax to pay. Where tax is payable, it is levied at 20 per cent on the top-slice – the amount over the higher tax threshold.

policies. This means a tiny element of life insurance is provided, typically adding just 1 per cent or less to the value of your investment after your death. Tax is levied on the underlying fund by HMRC and cannot be reclaimed. This makes bonds highly unsuitable – from a tax perspective at least – for non-taxpayers.

But for higher-rate taxpayers, the 5 per cent rule on income from policies is very attractive. With the 5 per cent rule, that higher-rate taxpayers can make regular withdrawals of up to that amount per year from their bond for 20 years, without being immediately liable to tax. This is because the income they receive is classed as return of capital by HMRC. Furthermore, if an investor does not use the 5 per cent withdrawal option in one year, he or she may take up to the previously foregone limit in subsequent years or any other variant, as long as the overall ceiling is not breached.

Even more significantly, this income is not added to an investor's other income for tax purposes, potentially benefiting elderly taxpayers whose pension income is taxable, subject to normal allowances.

WHAT ELSE CAN YOU INVEST IN?

Shares are not the only things you can invest in for the long term. Some other assets you are likely to come across, both in a fund or as a standalone investment, are described overleaf.

Corporate bonds: These are effectively IOUs issued by companies looking to borrow money for set periods. In return, they promise to pay a certain rate of interest each year until the bond matures.

The price of a corporate bond can move up or down in the same way as shares do. This is because a bond paying a certain rate of interest that may have seemed low a year or so ago will look more attractive if interest rates are falling sharply. Consequently there will greater demand for it, pushing up the price. Conversely, if rates rise, the value of a bond that pays a low rate of interest is likely to fall.

Generally, but not always, bonds are regarded as lower risk investments than shares, especially those from businesses where the company itself is not considered to be at risk even if profits suffer in a bad year. However, at a time when all share prices are falling and company failure rates are high, bond prices may also fall on fears that a business may not be able to service its bond debts.

Corporate bonds are generally available within collective or mutual funds, such as unit trusts. The funds' managers will buy and sell them in order to generate the most income with the lowest possible risk – subject to that fund's mandate. Although bonds are regarded as income-producing investments, many savers hold them for their growth prospects, reinvesting the income instead.

Government gilts: Gilts (or gilt-edged stocks) are bonds issued by the Government and they pay a fixed rate of interest twice a year. Like corporate bonds, they are bought and sold on the stock market where their price can go up or down. They can be bought and sold through brokers, high street banks or through the Government's Debt Management Office (DMO), which produces information about buying gilts at www.dmo.gov.uk/.

top tip: for most investors, gilts usually form part of a collective investment, for example an income fund, whose priority is to deliver income rather than growth.

Gilts are considered safe investments as the Government is unlikely to go bust or to default on the interest payments. However, you are not guaranteed to get all your capital back under all circumstances.

Property: In recent years, property such as offices, factories and warehouses has also become an increasingly attractive place for people's money. If the economy is booming, there is more likely to be a high demand for commercial space. Rent reviews almost always lead to increases, in turn increasing the value of the investment itself.

Until late 2007, commercial property was seen as a relatively secure investment. But in the 12 months that followed, the value of commercial property fell sharply and has remained low since then. Investors have discovered a fundamental downside to it: it is very illiquid, which means you can't sell it very easily.

The way to invest in commercial property is usually through a collective investment such as unit and investment trusts.

Commodities: At its simplest, a commodity is a physical substance – metal, oil, agricultural produce – that is traded in a number of international exchanges. Investors can also buy shares in companies that are engaged in the exploration and exploitation of those commodities, including producers.

Commodity investment has become increasingly popular in recent years, as global growth, led by the new economic powerhouse of China and, to a lesser extent, India, increased demand and pushed up prices. One of the claimed advantages of commodities is that they show little correlation to other main asset classes over the period, which means that they do not rise or fall in tandem with other shares.

Unlike bonds, commodities are real assets and tend to hold their value in the face of inflation. Similarly, they are physically scarce and, as such, can rise at times when other asset classes, such as shares, are falling. However, if the world economy suffers, demand for commodities falls rapidly, as was seen with the price of oil, which dropped from $150 a barrel in mid-2008 to less than $50 some nine months later.

Tracker funds: Trackers attempt to track the performance of an index such as the FTSE 100 or the All-Share, rather than set out to beat it. Tracker fund managers claim that no traditional manager manages to do better than the index for very long and, if that is so, it makes more sense to literally track the index.

How they do this differs between funds. Some trackers buy shares in all the companies that make up the index. Others use complex financial instruments to track what the index does by buying shares in a cross-section of companies.

In contrast with actively managed funds, trackers cost a fraction in annual management charges – usually less than 1 per cent a year and a fund manager will generally levy at least 1.5 per cent a year.

Tracker funds remain controversial because some experts argue that in a recession, when stock-picking skills assume greater importance, trackers are far more likely to drop down the performance league table. Moreover, IFAs argue that the 'average' funds that trackers beat is not a true average, because they consist of many poorly managed funds, which most of them would not be recommending to investors.

Hedge funds: A hedge fund will invest money in anything that it believes will make a profit. To achieve this, they operate in a far less restricted investment environment than traditional managers, such as investing in bankrupt or merging companies, or taking 'buy' or 'sell' positions on the direction of entire markets, currencies and commodities.

Although in recent years many hedge fund managers have been described as mainly attractive to sophisticated investors, in reality a good manager offers the potential to achieve investment returns with relatively low volatility and largely unrelated to whether a particular investment market is rising or falling. This is because hedge fund managers generally try to remove some market exposure by making an offsetting bet to hedge against losing money on the original investment position.

Even so, hedge funds can still lose money for themselves and their clients, or provide just rather disappointing returns, so choosing the right ones is key. For any investor keen on hedge funds, the advice is generally to use a proportion of their assets to spice up their portfolios.

CHOOSING THE RIGHT FUND

In addition to contemplating your attitude to risk and how a fund will fit with your goals, it is important to assess its performance before investing in it.

Most funds tend to promote themselves by publishing figures based on the past 12 months, three and five years' performance. In reality, this approach takes little account of volatility of a fund and by looking at fixed periods in this way it does not tell you whether a fund manager is consistently good. So here are some other things to consider.

Relative and absolute performance

Look at returns on a month-by-month basis, both in absolute terms and, more importantly, relative to a benchmark such as the FTSE All-Share index of UK companies, or a more specialist index where appropriate. If this is not possible, look at figures on an annual basis. This information is usually available directly from the fund manager and will tell you whether the fund has dipped in any one year or longer and, if examined against a benchmark, whether this was common among its peers.

Career record

Fund managers are increasingly prone to switching jobs. It may be necessary to look not so much at a fund but the manager's performance with different funds, including the one you are looking at. Citywire, an online investor information website (www.citywire.co.uk), assesses fund performance in this way.

Performance against risk

As often as not, unsuccessful investing results from investors picking funds that don't suit their investment needs. There are several websites with tools that allow private and institutional investors to find funds that can meet their needs. They include Lipper Hindsight's (www.lipperweb.com), Standard & Poor's (www.standardandpoor.com), FT Fund Ratings (www.ft.com) and Morningstar (www.morningstar.com).

INVESTMENT STRATEGY

If it is true that markets can move down as well as up (and sometimes sideways for long periods of time), how do you deal with setbacks and what strategies are there to minimise risks? Here are some ideas to bear in mind.

Diversify

Many people make the mistake of believing that because they have invested in several funds or have a small portfolio of shares, it shows they are spreading their risks widely. In fact, this may not be the case.

Regardless of who the manager is, many funds will often invest not just in the same sector but in the same companies. So make sure you ask your adviser to recommend funds where the investment style of each manager is distinct – as well as complementary – to each other.

Aim to create a portfolio where different types of assets – shares, fixed interest investments and so on – are affected differently by changes in the economy.

Use asset allocation models

Wealth management firms break down asset classes into four main categories: shares, fixed interest (such as bonds and government gilts), property and cash. The aim is to hold a percentage of your investments in each of these assets, with the precise amount determined by how long you are planning to invest for and your tolerance of risk.

Know your manager

Some managers may be 'interventionist', buying and selling shares regularly. Others may favour a buy-and-hold approach, where they aim to give a share more time to show how it can perform.

There may also be differences in terms of what investment approach a manager uses. There are two main ones:

'Value' investors: These concentrate on the fundamentals of a business. The manager will analyse the balance sheet and profit and loss account of a company, produce a valuation and compare it with the share price. A buy or sell decision is based on this 'bottom-up' approach.

'Growth' investors: Such investors make value judgements about a business, its markets, its management, and its ability to extract future earnings growth from its industry. A growth investor is likely to be more open to risk and will be willing to follow his or her instincts.

Don't try to time the market

It is always tempting to tell yourself that the market is not doing well right now and you will wait until it recovers before investing. But if you believe shares offer better long-term potential than cash deposits, this could be a mistake.

Share price rallies tend to be sudden and unpredictable, with the greatest rises happening in just a few days. Research published in November 2008 by the investment group Fidelity on the performance of the FTSE All-Share index over the past 20 years, found that investors who missed out on only the ten best-performing days in the market would have ended up with a portfolio worth roughly 39 per cent less than one that had been fully invested throughout the period.

Conversely, missing the ten worst performing days would have enhanced an investor's returns by 60 per cent. But would you – or anyone – have spotted any of those ten days in question?

Consider 'pound cost averaging'

When markets are volatile, most people don't like the idea of pumping large lump sums into shares that may fall suddenly the next day. One way round it is to invest smaller amounts more regularly – pound cost averaging. It means that when a market is falling, you can buy more shares (or units) with the same money, and vice versa when the market is rising.

Of course, every transaction costs money in brokers' commissions and Stamp Duty, so periodic small purchases of individual shares don't work well. But if you adopt pound cost averaging through a unit or investment trust, these costs can be less.

top tip: pound cost averaging is not meant to be a mechanism for making more money, but it helps even out some of the potential sharp losses when and if markets are falling.

Review regularly

One of the things many investors forget is the need to constantly re-examine how their assets are changing over time. This is important, whether stocks are falling or rising.

When stocks are falling, review them to ensure your portfolio is positioned in a defensive manner. This might mean moving out of technology shares and into, say, tobacco stocks or food retailers, or switching from an emerging market fund into one focusing on high income-yielding shares.

When stocks are rising, review them to ensure you have a balanced portfolio that straddles a wide range of assets in the UK and abroad.

Most important, if you skew your holdings in one direction, ensure it is a conscious decision, not an accidental one you may regret later.

Cut your losses

Although there are powerful arguments in favour of long-term strategic asset allocation, there will be occasions when that particular approach comes under strong challenge. Sharply falling stock markets is one example, particularly when individual funds or company shares are not performing well.

Although the general advice to investors is never to panic in the face of a downturn, there will be times when you should make considered and rational decisions, which may well involve selling up and switching your money elsewhere.

Aim for dividends

One way to maximise returns is to invest in shares (and funds) where you stand a chance of earning a reasonable dividend.

When a company makes a profit, it can use that money in two main ways: it can either reinvest it in the business, or it can be paid to the shareholders as a dividend. Many companies do a mixture of both. This is usually set as a fixed amount per share, so shareholders can work out how much of a dividend they are likely to receive based on the number of shares they own.

For many investors, dividend-paying shares are a way of achieving stock market exposure while still receiving a reasonable income from their portfolios. But dividends are not just for income-seekers. If reinvested, as they often are, they form an important part of total returns for investors.

The importance of dividends is illustrated by research in the annual Barclays Equity-Gilt study. The latest report, published early in 2009, has found the gains from dividends make all the difference in terms of share price performance. Had you invested £100 in equities at the end of 1945 with dividends reinvested, that money would be worth £131,000 now. By contrast, £100 in a savings account would be only be worth £5,789.

Details of companies and their dividend yields are available in newspapers like the *Financial Times* and *The Times*, or their websites (www.ft.com and www.timesonline.co.uk). They can also be found on investment sites, such as Interactive Investor (www.iii.co.uk).

Investing free of tax

For millions of investors, saving money is difficult. Doing so in a situation where you have to pay tax on your nest egg would be even worse. Thankfully, there are rules that ensure all but a minority of savers do not have to pay tax on their investments.

INDIVIDUAL SAVINGS ACCOUNTS

Aside from pensions (see pages 142–56), the primary method to invest your money free of tax is in an Individual Savings Account (ISA).

If you are 50 or over on 5 April 2010, from 6 October 2009, you can invest up to £10,200 in ISA accounts annually. The full amount may be invested in a stocks and shares ISA, or you can invest up to £5,100 (£3,600 prior to 6 October 2009) in a cash ISA and the balance in a stocks and shares ISA.

If you are 49 or under on 5 April 2010, you can invest up to £7,200 in ISA accounts overall during the 2009–10 tax year. The full amount may be invested in a stocks and shares ISA, or you can invest up to £3,600 in a cash ISA and the balance in a stocks and shares ISA. From 6 April 2010, you will be able to invest up to £10,200 in ISA accounts overall regardless of your age (so long as you are over 18) of which up to £5,100 can be held in a cash ISA.

Here are the basic rules.

To pay into an ISA you must be a UK resident or a Crown employee (such as diplomat) or a member of the armed forces (who is working overseas but paid by the Government), including husbands and wives or civil partners.
You must be aged over 16 years for the cash component, and over 18 years for stocks and shares.
An ISA is in a single name alone.

You can open one cash ISA and one stocks and shares ISA in each tax year. These can either be with a single ISA provider, or with two different providers.

ISA savings allowances are offered on a 'use it or lose it' basis: if you don't use up your annual allowance in the relevant tax year, you can't get it back the following year. And if you withdraw money from an ISA, you can't top it up again in the same tax-free environment.

You can transfer money saved in previous years' cash ISA holdings to stocks and shares ISAs without affecting your current year's allowance. You can also switch between cash ISA providers, as well as between shares ISAs. But once you switch from cash to a shares ISA, you cannot switch back to cash.

FRIENDLY SOCIETIES

Friendly Societies offer the means to shelter a small additional tax-free sum in their investment plans, over and above what can be placed into a pension or an ISA.

Although often ignored by many investors, Friendly Societies have been around for hundreds of years. They grew from the simple premise that if a group of people contributed to a mutual fund, then they could receive benefits at a time of need.

There are still about 200 Friendly Societies, with millions of customers, offering long-term savings schemes up to a maximum contribution limit of £25 a month or £270 a year. The money usually goes into with-profits funds, which invest in a combination of shares, bonds and property.

top tip: despite their quaint names, some societies can boast excellent high-performing funds. In some cases, their financial strength is greater than household name firms such as Standard Life or Norwich Union/Aviva.

Saving in these schemes can be a good idea if you are prepared to sit out an investment, but they can have high charges and heavy penalties if the product is surrendered early. (For more information, see the Friendly Societies website at www.friendlysocieties.co.uk.)

CHILD TRUST FUNDS

For many people, one investment goal is to help provide for their children, for which a Child Trust Fund (CTF) is worth considering. A CTF is a tax-free savings and investment account for children, with three main aims:

● To help children learn about the importance of saving money
● To encourage parents (and relatives) to save for their children
● To build up a nest egg that children can then use to help fund themselves through college, or in the first years after leaving school.

The main rules of CTFs are:

That parents of every child born on or after 1 September 2002 receive a voucher worth £250 from the Government. This rises to £500 for families that qualify for full Child Tax Credit.
If you do not open an account with the voucher you are sent, HMRC will do so on your behalf, opening a stakeholder account (see overleaf).
The Government then pays a further £250 to every child when they become seven years of age.
In addition, parents, relatives and friends can contribute up to £1,200 a year into the fund, which grows free of tax until maturity.
The money is there to be invested on a child's behalf in a special fund and the account is managed by a parent or guardian until the child reaches the age of 16 years.
Once a child turns 16, he or she becomes the registered contact. Annual statements are sent direct to him or her and the account can be moved to a different provider or its type changed. Once aged 18, the young adult has access to the money to use as he or she thinks best.

Choice of CTFs

Anyone investing in a CTF will have a choice of three accounts.

Savings accounts: With a savings account any money you invest is secure. For example, if you invest £500, your child will get that sum of money back as well as earning a level of interest between now and when the fund matures. In effect, your money will be saved in the same way as it would in a high-interest building society account. There are no explicit charges for a cash-based CTF: the provider's costs are met through an adjustment in the interest paid.

Stakeholder accounts: Stakeholder accounts invest your child's money in shares. However, a number of rules aim to reduce the risk of investing in shares and make these accounts more flexible and better value. Here are the main points of a stakeholder CTF:

Your child's money is invested among a number of company shares in order to reduce the risk.
Once the account is open, all providers must accept a minimum contribution of £10 into a stakeholder account – but they can accept less if they wish.
Charges on the stakeholder account are limited to 1.5 per cent a year, which means the charge can be no more than £1.50 for every £100 in the account. This limit does not apply to other types of CTF.
Once your child is 13, money in the account starts to be moved to lower risk investments, such as bonds. This is known as 'lifestyling' and aims to ensure that your child is not vulnerable to a sharp stock market fall just before the CTF matures, cutting the value of any final payout.

Stakeholder accounts are a default option for CTFs: if you do not open an account in your child's name within 12 months of receiving your voucher, the Government will place it in a stakeholder fund.

Share-based accounts: These accounts invest your child's money by buying shares in companies.
   The charges on this type of account are likely to be a percentage of the CTF's value and the research required to choose the right shares for a CTF will also be charged to you. You should find out from your chosen CTF provider how much this might be. Share-based CTFs generally charge an initial fee of 5 per cent of your investment, plus an annual management charge ranging between 1 and 1.5 per cent.

Switching CTFs
You cannot divide your money among different accounts, but you can switch between them, including cash to share-based CTFs and vice versa. There is no charge for doing so, although if you have stocks and

In the event of overpayment

With many CTF providers, if you exceed the £1,200 a year limit, they will place the money in a holding account and pay interest on it until the child's next birthday. The money is then transferred into the next year's CTF, subject to that annual limit, when it will automatically transfer into the account.

Not all providers will do this, so check first if you think the total of combined contributions will go over the limit.

The alternative is for you to set up an account into which contributions can be made before they reach the CTF annual maximum. In that way, any additional sums can be diverted into other tax-free savings products available at the time.

This type of account is sometimes called a 'feeder account', but any type of account that you can use to make regular penalty-free transfers into and from will do.

shares as part of a CTF account, your provider may charge you for the cost of selling them and there are sometimes penalties for moving your funds elsewhere.

To transfer your funds all that you need to do is sign up with a new provider who will let your old provider know. The new provider will inform HMRC so that any further government payments will go into the right account.

It may take two to three weeks for the transfer to take place – unless there are any associated penalties for switching. If this is the case, the decision on whether to move right away or wait is based on the penalties involved.

Persuading friends and family to save

One of the key attractions of a CTF is that potential contributors can include grandparents, relatives and friends.

Anyone can put money into your child's CTF account if they want to, but they would need to ask you, as the registered contact, for the account details in order to pay it in directly. They can then pay in as much or as little as they want, subject to the £100 a month/£1,200 annual cap.

(Continued on page 138)

Case study

Mike Barton, 42, and his wife Linda, 37, have assets of £75,000, held in a range of ISAs and other investments. Mike runs a fast food franchise with three branches in his local town and earns £65,000 a year. Linda is a company secretary and earns £18,000 a year. They have a £100,000 tracker mortgage on their property, at a rate of 4.7 per cent. The couple have very little pension provision, but recently inherited £325,000 following the death of Mike's mother.

Mike and Linda want to use the bulk of the inheritance to enhance their future retirement income, for when they stop work at the age of 60 years. Ideally, they would like to pay as little tax as possible, now and in the future. They would also prefer to have something set aside for their two children, Sarah and Karl, aged 5 and 3, when they go to university. The couple have a 'moderate' attitude towards risk: they are prepared to invest in shares, but do not want to take excessive risks with their money.

Goals

- To set aside as much money as is reasonably possible for Mike and Linda's future pension needs.
- To pay as little tax as possible.
- To set up an investment fund for Sarah and Karl.

Plan

- By paying off £100,000 of their mortgage, Mike and Linda are effectively 'earning' 4.7 per cent tax free on their investment, freeing up more of their monthly income either to invest or to enhance their lifestyle.
- Sarah and Karl were born after September 2002 and are both young enough to qualify for their own CTFs, into which Mike and Linda can contribute up to £1,200 a year – or £100 a month – for each CTF. The money set aside will roll up free of tax and mature when each child reach 18 years of age. If Mike and Linda set aside that money, plus a further £25 a month into a Friendly Society savings plan for each child, they will ensure they are well provided for when and if they go to college.
- Mike and Linda also have the option of saving into either a pension or ISA. Both offer tax-free benefits: a pension offers tax relief on any sum invested, while the income is taxed (see Chapter 8). ISA contributions are made on taxed earnings, but the income received is tax free. An added incentive for ISAs is that any sums saved in one can be passed on to dependents, albeit subject to Inheritance Tax. This is not quite as easy with a pension.
- Before April 2010, Mike and Linda can save £7,200 each in stocks and shares ISAs, a total of £14,400. After 5 April 2010, they can save £10,200 each in their respective ISAs, a total of £34,800. The couple may also wish to create a 'feeder' account (see page 135) for the 2011–12 tax year, into which they place

a further £20,400. Although this feeder account will be subject to tax, when the money is subsequently paid into the ISA future gains will be free of tax, as will income paid when they need it at age 60. To reduce tax liabilities, the feeder account should be in Linda's name only, as she is subject to tax at 20 per cent, whereas Mike would have to pay 40 per cent on his share of the account. The total new money in Mike and Linda's ISAs would then be £55,200.

● Mike and Linda are not currently making contributions into a pension scheme. They can pay up to 100 per cent of their earnings into a personal pension, which would entitle them to pay in a total of £83,000 in the 2009–10 tax year and the same in 2010–11, subject to their earnings remaining at the same level. If so, they could invest up to £166,000 over the two tax years, or £249,000 if they place the remainder of their money into the same high-interest feeder account as with their future ISA contributions.

● In the case of both pensions and ISAs, the key is not so much the investment vehicle they are investing in but the asset allocation strategy they are considering. A typical growth portfolio for moderate risk investors would divide assets in the following way: 55 per cent equities, 4 per cent high-yielding (and therefore slightly riskier) bonds, 23 per cent in investment grade bonds, 15 per cent other assets (such as commercial property) and 3 per cent cash.

● This asset allocation should be considered jointly, across both Mike and Linda's combined pension and new ISA portfolios, including their existing ISAs and other saving schemes. Further professional advice needs to be sought in terms of how to divide the equity side of their portfolio, both with regard to geographical diversification and also the size of companies their funds will invest in – with the bulk of their funds going into so-called 'large cap' shares of major UK and overseas companies.

● If Mike and Linda prefer not to pay tax even at the expense of higher savings rates, they could shelter up to £15,000 each in fixed interest certificates, as well as index-linked savings certificates with National Savings & Investments (NS&I). In July 2009 these paid a maximum of 1.9 per cent for the five-year fixed interest scheme or RPI plus 1 per cent of the index-linked scheme. This is not an especially high rate, but would be the equivalent of 3.17 per cent before tax in Mike's case and 2.38 per cent for Linda. If they were to opt for NS&I investments, they could then consider reducing the cash component in other parts of their overall investment portfolio.

The above are only possibilities: in considering any investment scenario, as well which tax-free savings vehicle to place their money, Mike and Linda should consult with an IFA.

For stakeholder CTFs, contributions can be paid in cash, cheque, standing order and direct debit. For non-stakeholder accounts, it will be up to the individual financial providers as to how they choose to accept payments.

Bereavement and terminal illness

If your child dies, his or her money will be returned to you in full. This applies both in the case of death or terminal illness. More details on how to do this can be found on the Government's CTF website: www.childtrustfund.gov.uk.

OTHER TAX-FREE INVESTMENT PRODUCTS FOR CHILDREN

CTFs are not the only way to save money on your child's behalf in a tax-free environment. Other options include:

ISAs (see page 131): A CTF can only be cashed by your child at the age of 18 years, but with an ISA you can access the money relatively quickly in an emergency.

Stakeholder pensions (see page 156): Again, the underlying tax treatment is the same as a CTF. The key advantage of a long-term pension scheme like this is that a lump sum paid in now will grow over 50 or more years. Compound growth could mean a retiree will receive a very large amount of money for no effort, long after your death. The main difference is that your child is unable to access the money until he or she is 55 years old.

Friendly Society bonds (see page 132): Each child has a tax-free Friendly Society allowance of £270 a year.

NS&I Children's Bonus Bonds: These is an investment limit of £3,000 in each issue of bonds, with new issues being launched each time interest rates change, on average up to four times a year. They are held in the name of the child, under the control of a parent or guardian until the child is 16, the bonds can be opened with as little as £25. The bonds can be left to mature until a child is 21 years of age.

8: Maximising your pension

Planning for your financial future will make a big difference to the amount of income you can look forward to in retirement – and even seemingly small amounts of money can help you build up that nest egg.

- **Making a plan**
- **The State Pension system**
- **Occupational pension schemes**
- **Other forms of pension**
- **Converting pension into income**
- **Women and pensions**
- **Long-term care**
- **Equity release**

Making a plan

The UK population is rapidly getting older – and the impact on everyone's retirement is likely to become greater as a result.

Declining levels of mortality for people over retirement age mean that a man of 65 can expect to live another 16.6 years and a woman of the same age another 19.4 years. In turn, the proportion of people aged 65 and over is projected to increase from 16 per cent in 2006 to 22 per cent by 2031.

This matters because the UK's pension system is largely based on the premise that one person's retirement income – the element that comes from the state at least – requires several people of working age to pay for it through their taxes. Yet, as the proportion of older people increases, that of people in work is beginning to fall. As time passes, successive governments will be less able to offer substantial pensions to those who reach retirement age, so it is important to make a plan for your retirement.

Work out exactly when you want to retire and how much income you are likely to need.

Calculate how much you may receive from the state at 65 (or later, if your assumed retirement date is after 2024) (see pages 142–4).

Add any additional pensions or investments from all other quarters, including both work-related schemes and private plans.

Work out what the missing amount is between what you expect to receive and what you want.

Come up with a plan to help you bridge that gap and act on it.

HOW MUCH WILL YOU NEED?

Most of us don't really know how much we will actually need to live on when we finally stop work. But knowing what to aim for is critical: a notional target allows you to consider two aspects of your planning.

Should you save more now to live better later? Is it better to scale down what can sometimes be grandiose ideas about the future – round-the-world cruises and country cottages – and simply enjoy life now?

There is no cut-and-dried answer to either question. Or rather, the answer will lie somewhere along a scale that only you can determine.

Many IFAs give their clients a rough-and-ready figure of between half and two thirds of current take-home income in order to maintain a similar lifestyle to the one they do now.

Budgeting for the future

To be more precise about your annual and monthly needs, you will need to add – and deduct – costs from your budget. Here's how:

Assume an ideal monthly income, after tax, that would allow you to pay all your major bills today, including Council Tax, telephone, heating and electricity. Your current income (combined with your partner's income if you are in a relationship) may not be relevant in this respect.
Do not include any mortgage payments you currently make from the likely income, as you will in all probability have paid the mortgage off.
Add the cost of an annual holiday (divided by 12 months), a couple of meals out every month or so, plus a monthly clothes budget. Include car maintenance costs (also divided by 12), running repairs to the house and so on. You may take up a hobby, so add an amount for that.
By the time you retire, you should no longer have to offer financial support to your children. So deduct those costs.
Take off the monthly cost of commuting, the suits and dry-cleaning bills, the takeaway lunches and canteen coffees.
Deduct the monthly amount you save into a pension or other savings.
If you are planning to downsize, moving to a smaller/cheaper property and using the spare capital for income, calculate roughly the amount of equity you hope to release by such a step. Assume an income of about 4 or 5 per cent from any lump sum you may have left over after downsizing. If you are likely to receive any inheritances in the next 20–30 years, add those too, as you may choose to receive an income from some or all of that lump sum too.

You will now have arrived at a monthly figure you need to live on when you retire. Multiply that by 12 and you have an annual income.

The State Pension system

There are several elements of state support that you will receive, based on your total earnings, National Insurance contributions (NICs) and any savings you manage to build up between now and retirement. Here are the most important ones.

BASIC STATE PENSION

State Pensions are currently paid at 65 for men and 60 for women. Over a ten-year period, starting on 6 April 2010, women's pension ages will gradually be raised to 65.

In addition, the State Pension age for both men and women is then set to increase from 65 to 68 between April 2024 and April 2046, with each additional year being phased in over two consecutive years in each decade. So, the State Pension age for men and women will increase to 66 in April 2024, to 67 in April 2034 and 68 in April 2044. Each rise will be phased in over two years. If you were born after April 1976, you will be 68 when you retire.

Not everyone will receive the maximum State Pension. It is based on the number of 'qualifying years' of NICs that you have paid or been treated as paying. After April 2010, both sexes will need 30 qualifying years for their full State Pension, with people receiving 1/30th of the full basic State Pension for each qualifying year they have. So if, for example, you have ten qualifying years, you would be entitled to 10/30ths of the full basic State Pension. There is no longer a minimum qualifying period.

In 2009–10 the full basic State Pension is £95.70 a week for a single person and £152.30 a week for couples. This is uprated in line with inflation, so assuming a future government does not abandon this pledge that is roughly what you can expect to get when you retire.

If you put off claiming your State Pension, you can either receive an extra income or a one-off taxable lump sum payment. This income is calculated as an extra 1 per cent for every five weeks you put off claiming, equivalent to about 10.4 per cent extra for each year.

Alternatively, if you don't claim for at least 12 consecutive months, you can choose to receive a taxable one-off lump sum payment instead and have your State Pension paid at the normal rate. The lump sum payment, when you claim it, will be based on the amount of normal weekly State Pension you would have received, plus interest added each week and compounded.

STATE SECOND PENSION

Since April 2002, those who reach retirement age can receive a new additional State Second Pension (S2P), which is earnings-related. S2P is a pension top-up scheme, payable to all employees – as long as they are not opted or contracted out of the scheme by their employers.

The way S2P is calculated is very complicated, but it is based on the number of years you have been contracted into the scheme when you reach State Pension age.

Payments are based on a proportion of your earnings each year between a lower- and upper-earnings limit. A rough calculation for those who have never contracted out would be 20 per cent of earnings above £4,680 per year, but less than £40,040 per year.

After 2012, the way payments are calculated will change again. The aim is to ensure that payouts favour those on lower incomes – anyone earning less than £13,500 in the 2008–09 tax year will be treated as if they earn as much as that amount when it comes to their build-up of S2P retirement income.

Opting in or out of S2P

Until now it has been possible for employees to opt in or out of the S2P, whether individually or as part of their employers' pension scheme. After 2012 it will no longer be possible to opt out. Until then, if you are thinking of opting in or out, consider:

Contracting out exposes you to investment risk: Experts calculate that you would need to achieve annual returns of between 7 and 14 per cent on the rebates invested in your personal plan to match the S2P. At the same time, the annuity you buy with this fund when you retire may be less than you expected. On the other hand, all government pensions are subject to tampering by successive parties in office, which means there is a political risk associated with continued membership of S2P.

Your age: Any rebate is capped when you reach the age of 53 years. Therefore, the advice of most life insurers is that at that age you should be thinking about opting back into S2P if you had previously opted out.

Your income: If you are on a low income, the benefits from S2P are far greater than contracting out.

Inheritance: If you contract out of S2P and die before you start taking your private pension, your fund will be used to buy a pension for your husband or wife. If you are not married, there is no fund to be paid to your estate, so your dependents could lose out.

Early retirement: since April 2006, you can take your private pension from the age of 50 (rising to 55 in 2010) and up to 25 per cent of your fund as a tax-free lump sum. If you stay in S2P, you will not be able to receive a weekly pension until you reach the State Pension age.

PENSION CREDIT

Pension Credit is a new form of pension top-up, aimed at people who reach retirement age, but have limited income other than their basic State Pension. Pension Credit is in addition to the basic State Pension and increases income to a guaranteed minimum of £130 a week if you are single or £198.45 for couples. However, what you get is reduced in proportion to any other pension you receive or savings you may have.

The deduction made for other pensions or other income, such as ISAs, is 40p for every £1 of income you receive each week. For example, if you are entitled to a full State Pension of £95.70 a week and also receive a pension of £20 a week from a former employer, that income would see your combined State Pension and Pension Credit reduced by £8 a week, from £130 a week to £122.

The deductions made for lump sum savings is calculated at a rate of £1 a week for every £500 of capital above £10,000. For example, someone with £15,000 in the bank would lose £10 a week.

Occupational pension schemes

Implicit in the State's relatively limited pension system is the assumption that for many, perhaps most, pensioners there will be additional sources of income in retirement that can enhance the basic amount they receive from the Government.

For millions of people in the UK, that additional source of income is likely to be an employer's occupational pension scheme. Although their availability has been severely dented in recent years by claims of high costs and of inflexibility by employers offering them, up to 12 million people in the UK remain eligible for a company pension.

Contributing to a final salary scheme has important tax advantages. Employees' and their employers' contributions into a pension enjoy tax relief. If you are a 20 per cent taxpayer, for every £80 you pay into a pension, HMRCs adds a further £20. If you are a higher-rate taxpayer, for every £60, HMRC pays in £40.

There are two main types of company scheme: final salary and money purchase pensions.

FINAL SALARY PENSIONS
These schemes are also described as 'defined benefits', because what staff may receive is agreed at the outset. Employees pay a fixed amount of their salary into the pension scheme every month. At retirement, the employee's pension is based on their final salary and linked to their years of service. The pension is generally linked to the retail price index (RPI), up to a maximum of 5 per cent and dependents' benefits are generally payable.

The most important difference between schemes is the number of years employees have to work before they are entitled to a full pension.

This is known as the accrual rate and is calculated on the basis of a fractional payment for each year of service. There are many different permutations of such schemes, depending on the employer.

For example, if you are in a 60ths scheme and complete 23 years service just before reaching your normal retirement age and your final pensionable salary is £70,000, you will receive a pension of: $(23 \times 70,000)/60 = £26,833$ a year.

A second factor that impacts on the eventual size of a final salary pension is how that final salary is calculated: some are based on the last year in work, while others will be linked to the final three years, or even a career average.

Final salary schemes are good if you spend most or all of your career with one employer. Promotion should mean your salary rises faster than inflation, boosting your pension at retirement. However, if you change jobs frequently, you will have to start all over again with each employer.

Final salary schemes rely on a combination of future stock market returns and ongoing company contributions to meet their guarantees to those coming up to retirement. If your employer goes bust, your pension is protected by a special Pension Protection Fund (PPF) paid for by contributions from other occupational schemes. But higher earners may not get back every penny.

The future of final salary pensions

In recent years, the popularity of these schemes among employers has declined dramatically, as they become increasingly reluctant to bear steeply rising costs and have to deal with what they see as complicated and onerous rules and regulations.

The situation has been made worse by a combination of serious underfunding of their own schemes by many employers in recent years, coupled with sustained falls in equity values plus ever-increasing costs created by longer life expectancy, which means that more needs to be set aside to fund staff retirement incomes.

As a result, recent research by the National Association of Pension Funds, shows increasing numbers of employers in the private sector have now closed their final salary occupational schemes to new staff. Some are also closing them to existing staff and placing them into new arrangements, such as money purchase pensions, described opposite.

MONEY PURCHASE PENSIONS

These schemes are also known as 'defined contributions', because the employer knows in advance how much it will pay into the fund. Both employer and employee pay an agreed amount into a fund each month, often between 5 and 10 per cent of the annual salary. The money is invested in stocks and shares, as well as bonds and other assets. At retirement, the employee's pot of money is used to buy an annuity, giving an annual income for life.

At retirement, that money is used to buy an annuity, or annual income for life, typically rising by a certain percentage each year, with additional payments to the deceased's spouse in the event of the main pension holder's death.

Money purchase schemes are good if you plan on switching jobs regularly. You can build up much more transparent retirement funds and sometimes have a greater choice over how your money is invested. On the other hand, they are bad for employees whose employers don't make generous contributions into their pension pots. Surveys show that most companies don't: figures from the Office for National Statistics (ONS) in 2008 revealed that money purchase schemes had an average contribution rate of just 2.7 per cent from staff and 6.5 per cent from employers. Experts agree this is not enough to purchase a significant pension at retirement for most employees. Final salary schemes, by contrast, had average contribution rates of 4.9 per cent from members and 15.6 per cent from employers.

top tip: it is possible not to join a company pension scheme. This will save you having to make any monthly contribution, but you forego your employer's own contributions.

Investing in the stock market means the value of a pension fund suffers if markets fall. Also, the fund is then used to buy an annuity and the rates for these are based on what is happening to government gilt yields, to which they are loosely linked (see pages 157–9): if these are low, so will the amount an annuity provider is prepared to offer you in annual income for your lump sum.

TOPPING UP A COMPANY PENSION

If you belong to a company scheme, you may feel that as long as you make regular payments into it – and your employer does the same – you will enjoy a decent income when you finally stop work. Unfortunately, for all bar the minority of people who stay with the same company for 30 or 40 years, a company pension will probably not be enough to fund a comfortable retirement. The only way to overcome this is to increase contributions into a pension.

By law, all companies offering a pension scheme to their employees must offer the facility to make additional contributions, even if they don't add more money themselves. HMRC rules stipulate that the maximum contribution an employee can make is 15 per cent of annual salary.

Additional voluntary contribution (AVC)

These contributions are used to buy 'added years' that are counted towards your retirement. For example, an additional contribution of 10 per cent of salary payable for a year might buy an extra year of service in a final salary scheme. More commonly, they are invested in a fund running alongside the main occupational scheme and are used to buy an annuity at retirement. You sometimes have a choice as to which fund your AVC contributions will go.

Free-standing additional voluntary contribution (FSAVC)

Alternatively, it is possible to set up FSAVCs, a private top-up scheme. The principle is the same as an AVC, except that you get to choose the pension fund your money will go into. In addition, an FSAVC is portable;

when you go to a new employer, you can continue making contributions into the FSAVC up to your 15 per cent limit.

Which is better?

Generally, most experts recommend that you should stick with a company AVC because the management fee of an AVC is almost always cheaper than its private counterpart.

In some cases, while not actually contributing to the AVC scheme directly, the employer will subsidise its management costs, sometimes paying for them altogether. Even if this is not the case, with most AVC top-up schemes you would expect to pay no more than 0.75 per cent in annual fees. By contrast, FSAVCs tend to be more expensive, with annual management charges in the 1 to 1.5 per cent range.

The freedom to choose your fund is often presented as a key reason to go for an FSAVC instead. In practice, however, surveys show that people who opt for FSAVCs don't choose 'adventurous' investment options; they tend allow their financial advisers to replicate the same asset mix as a company AVC.

As for the argument that FSAVCS are more portable, when you retire you are unlikely to have forgotten that for, say, five years as an employee you were also making contributions into an AVC.

SALARY SACRIFICE

Many people find that as they approach retirement it becomes increasingly important for them to save as much money as they can into a pension scheme. If so, salary sacrifice can be a way round the issue.

This is where you agree a reduced salary with your employer in exchange for extra pension contributions being paid to an occupational pension scheme. The advantage to you is that the employer's contribution receives the same tax relief as your own payments into the scheme. You can take a larger tax-free lump sum at retirement. You also benefit from inflation proofing of your pension after retirement (usually up to 5 per cent). A salary sacrifice reduces your pensionable earnings for maximum retirement benefits, your death in service benefits (such as life cover) and a dependent's pension.

Most significantly, from the employer's perspective, it means there is no need to pay NICs on the salary sacrificed. Not all employers offer salary sacrifice schemes. However, they may be willing to consider one.

TAX-FREE LUMP SUM

When an occupational pension is taken at retirement, you can take part of it as a tax-free lump sum – the cash commutation option. Since 6 April 2006, you can do this with any pension arrangement.

For money purchase schemes, you can take up to 25 per cent of the fund value at retirement. The balance is used to buy an annuity. **For final salary schemes,** there is no identifiable fund, so a complicated formula is used to calculate how much you can take, based on a multiple of your final pension at retirement.

Many schemes have commutation factors that are low, so you are not necessarily going to receive more money over your retirement by choosing to take the income rather than the tax-free cash.

Case study

Brian Patrick, 44, and his wife Martine, 36, would like to retire at 60, with an annual income worth 50 per cent of their combined salary.

A fleet car manager with annual earnings of £41,000, Brian has a paid-up final salary occupational pension scheme from an earlier job between the ages of 22 and 31, when he left on an income of £29,000. He has also built up a further money purchase pension pot worth £35,000 through his current company scheme, into which he pays 10 per cent and his employer pays in 5 per cent of earnings.

Martine, a midwife who joined the NHS at 20, earns £32,000. She sees herself staying in the Health Services until retirement. The couple's combined ISA investments and other savings are worth £45,000.

Goals

● To work out what their existing pension entitlements might be at retirement.
● To determine the size of any funding gap.
● To assess how this gap might best be bridged.
● To re-assess if the likely cost of bridging the funding gap is not possible.

Plan

● Assuming he decides not to take a tax-free lump sum, Brian's paid-up 1/60th final salary pension will be worth £5,220 a year if he retires at 60 or £6,525 if he retires at 65. This is because there is a 20 per cent reduction in income for taking his pension five years early.

OCCUPATIONAL PENSION SCHEME PROTECTION

For many years, people who contributed into occupational pension schemes risked losing a large proportion of their funds if their employer went bust. The law set out a complicated set of rules, in which the only ones who received reasonably generous protection in such cases were those who had already retired.

For those who might have left their employment and were now working elsewhere, or who had spent many years with the same company, or were potentially just months away from retirement, the law was much less generous. In some cases, they risked receiving only a fraction of their anticipated income.

In April 2005, the Pension Protection Fund (PPF) was set up for all companies that became insolvent after that date and provided final salary pension scheme benefits. The PPF aims to top up the entitlement

---

- Based on continued employer and employee pension contributions into his money purchase scheme between now and his chosen retirement age of 60, plus his tax-free ISA and other investments, Brian's combined pension lump sum would be worth about £270,000, taking inflation into account. Fund growth is assumed to be 7 per cent a year between now and his chosen retirement date. The total projected income would be about £10,200. If he chose to retire at 65, his combined income would rise to about £15,000.
- Martine's occupational pension is part of the NHS, which has a 1/80th accrual rate, plus a payment of a lump sum. She will receive a pension worth 50 per cent of her salary on retirement at age 60. Or she may convert the lump sum into an extra pension. Based on current salary levels, she would be entitled to a pension worth about £20,000 a year.
- The current State Pension scheme pays £152 a week, or about £7,900 a year at age 65 to Martine and Brian.
- Based on the above, Brian and Martine's combined pension at 60 (also using their ISAs to date) would be about £35,400 at age 60. This is about 45 per cent of their combined current salary. At age 65, they will receive a further £7,900, comfortably putting them over their 50 per cent target.
- If Brian wishes to raise his retirement income to meet that 50 per cent target, he would need to increase monthly pension contributions from his current £341.67 level to about £649.17 a month, about £208 a month before tax relief.
- Alternatively, Martine could buy the additional income through her existing NHS scheme. This would cost her about £220 a month.

of its claimants to 90 per cent of their promised benefits up to £31,932 per year (from April 2009) if the claimant has not reached normal retirement age. If the PPF claimant did reach retirement age at the time of the insolvency, the benefit would be topped up to 100 per cent with no cut-off.

However, the PPF benefits are not quite as generous as they seem since inflation proofing only applies to benefits accrued after April 1997.

Some pension experts have suggested that if a typical final salary scheme is taken over by the PPF, the total value of PPF benefits might be of the order of 70 per cent of the scheme's own promised benefits. For more details about the PPF, check out its website: www. pensionprotectionfund.org.uk.

Your pension and living abroad

According to a recent survey, up to 50 per cent of us would like to retire abroad. If so, what happens to your pension?

State Pension: You can continue to receive a UK pension, sent to you by cheque, paid into a chosen non-UK bank account or paid to a designated agent on your behalf. However, annual index-linked increases of the UK state pension are only paid to those living in the European Economic Area and Switzerland, as well as countries where there are reciprocal social security agreements. This includes the US, Turkey, Bermuda, Mauritius, Philippines, the former republics of Macedonia or Bosnia-Herzegovina. But if you retire to Canada, Australia or South Africa, your pension will not rise in line with inflation.
Occupational pension schemes: Almost all pension schemes will want to pay your pension into a UK bank account. It is then up to you to transfer the money into your local (non-UK) bank, subject to whatever transfer fees may be charged for doing so.
Personal pensions: Similar rules apply.

The position in respect of pensions and your tax liabilities can be extremely complicated if you choose to live abroad. It makes sense, at the outset, to contact HMRC on 084 4209 3934.

Other forms of pension

Although millions of employees in the UK are covered by company pension schemes, many others are self-employed and are therefore not eligible to be members of one or they need another type of pension altogether. If this includes you, here are some options that might help.

PERSONAL PENSIONS

Another way to save more is through personal pensions. Although much maligned in recent years, they remain an essential part of long-term retirement planning.

A personal pension is a private money purchase-style savings scheme (see page 147), where money is paid into a fund, which is then invested. The proceeds are used to buy an annuity (a regular income) at retirement. Payments can be made either monthly or by means of a lump sum, usually at the end of a tax year, although the size of the contributions are based on limits determined by HMRC.

Retirement is allowed at any age between 55 and 75, although the earlier an annuity is bought, the smaller it will be because it has to be paid out for a longer period.

Anyone who is self-employed can take out a personal pension, as can employees where no company scheme is available; where some of the benefits are not applicable to their personal circumstances (what use is a dependents' pension if you are unmarried and without children?); or where the main scheme's investment strategy is massively out of kilter with your own (either on ethical or performance grounds).

The benefits of personal pensions are outlined overleaf.

Tax relief on the way in. For every £100 paid in, basic-rate taxpayers contribute £80. HMRC pays the remaining £20. Higher-rate taxpayers not only receive the same tax relief, but can also claim back an additional 20p for every pound of contributions when they fill in their tax forms. Or else they can offset this rebate against other earnings.
Money inside a pension fund rolls up free of tax.
Partial tax relief on the way out. When a personal pension is finally cashed in, a policyholder has the option to take up to 25 per cent of the final lump sum as tax-free cash, which includes HMRC's contribution.

But there are also two main downsides:

The income you receive from a pension is taxed. But equally, most higher-rate taxpayers revert to the basic rate after retirement, making pensions a very tax-efficient vehicle.
Annuities have to be bought with the pension pot by the age of 75. This can mean that if the annuitant dies shortly after taking out an annuity, his or her estate may not receive a penny of that pension pot. Again, there are ways around the issue (see pages 157–9).

Contributions limits
You can save up to the equivalent of your gross income to the following levels:
2009–10: £245,000
2010–11: £255,000.

However, you will only receive full tax relief up to your current income.
   If you do not have an income, you can still contribute up to £2,880 net (£3,600 gross) per annum and receive basic rate tax relief of 20 per cent. In the year before you take your benefits, there is no maximum contribution limit.

Lifetime allowances
There is also a maximum fund value that you can have in your pension plan:
2009–10: £1.75m
2010–11: £1.8m.

SPECIALIST PENSIONS

In addition to personal pensions, there are some more specialist schemes aimed at people with more specific requirements.

Self-Invested Personal Pension (SIPP)

SIPPs offer investors the option of making their own investment decisions and have a wider investment scope than traditional pension funds. SIPPs allow the pension holder to choose from such things as stocks and shares, including investment trust and open-ended investment company (OEIC) shares on any HMRC-recognised stock exchange, futures and options contracts, unit trusts and commercial property, including that of your own company.

It is this latter aspect of a SIPP that attracts many investors because if your partnership or company wants to buy a freehold commercial property, you can either use the existing SIPP funds to purchase the property outright, or put down a deposit of up to 50 per cent of all the assets in your SIPP pension and arrange the balance on a commercial mortgage. The property is owned by the pension fund and therefore any growth in its value is free of Income Tax or Capital Gains Tax (CGT). In addition, the rent payable by the partnership or company to the pension fund can be offset against your profits.

Remember, though, that any income you take from your pension in retirement is taxed. SIPPs often come with set-up costs of up to £500, plus additional annual charges of up to 1.5 per cent. This means they are more suitable for experienced investors who are confident about making their own decisions and have large portfolios to invest.

top tip: SIPPS are also good for Inheritance Tax (IHT) planning, as the whole of your SIPP fund can usually be paid as a cash sum, free of IHT as the benefit will be paid at the trustees' discretion.

Small Self-Administered Scheme (SSAS)

SSASs are aimed at directors of companies. They are ideal for small limited companies where the shares are mainly or wholly owned by working directors. Both the company and the beneficiary can make contributions. Setting up a SSAS involves complicated and potentially expensive arrangements. Both legal, actuarial and accountants' advice is strongly recommended.

Stakeholder pensions

These were introduced by the government in 2001. They are, in essence, an offshoot of personal pensions and work in exactly the same way. The only key distinguishing features of stakeholder schemes are that managers can only charge fees of up to 1.5 per cent of your pension fund each year for the first ten years, and up to 1 per cent thereafter.

You can start contributions from as little as £20, and pay weekly, monthly or at less regular intervals. You can stop, re-start or change your payments whenever you want without penalty fees and can also switch to a different provider without penalty. All employers with more than five employees must make a stakeholder scheme available to their staff unless they already have another scheme in place, although there are exemptions – and employers do not have to contribute into the schemes they provide. Stakeholder pensions can be set up without having to be in work, up to a maximum of £3,600 a year, and there are no age restrictions either. This means that parents can set up a pension for their children if they wish, although it can only be accessed at 55.

Boosting your retirement income through tax relief

You are allowed to set up a separate stakeholder pension scheme and contribute into it – in addition to your employer's pension – as long as you have another source of income in that tax year, no matter how small. For example, a Saturday job may be classed as a separate employment, entitling you to make an annual contribution of up to £3,600 into a stakeholder pension.

Converting pension into income

When you retire, you will probably have a number of potential sources of income: State Pension, a final salary scheme, a company money purchase scheme, a personal pension and AVCs and FSAVCs.

If you are on a final salary scheme, your company administrator will calculate the size of your pension upon retirement. If you are on a company money purchase scheme or have a personal pension, the level of pension depends on how much is in your savings pot, because it is with that money that you must buy an annuity to provide an annual income for the rest of your life.

THE SIZE OF AN ANNUITY

An annuity is a type of insurance policy that provides an income in exchange for a lump sum. On retiring and by the age of 75, you must convert the capital you have built up into an annuity, but up to 25 per cent of that pot may be taken as a tax-free lump sum. An annuity is based on three main factors:

The assumed longevity of the person buying one (a function of age, sex and health at the time of annuity purchase).
Long-term interest rates, based on gilt rates (the interest paid on long-dated government bonds).
The company you buy the annuity from.

As such, making the right decision here can make a difference of up to 30 per cent on the final income you can expect from your pension. Other considerations that will determine the amount payable each year are described overleaf.

If the annuity is to be uprated each year in line with inflation or to be paid at a flat or level rate. If it is to be uprated, the initial amount paid is lower but rises over the years.

Whether it is a single life pension, paid only to you, or a spouse's pension that continues to be paid on death of the main annuitant. You can choose any proportion of the original pension amount, up to 100 per cent, although the usual level is between one and two thirds of your pension. A dependent's pension paid after your death will reduce what you receive now.

Guaranteed payments, where the same level of pension will continue to be paid to your spouse or civil partner (or to your estate) at the same level after your death. You can ask for this guarantee to apply for up to ten years. The longer the guarantee, the less you will get now.

Frequency of income (monthly, quarterly or half-yearly). The more frequent the payment, the less you receive.

Whether this income is paid in advance or arrears: you get less if it is paid in advance.

Your health. Some people may receive larger annuities, also known as impaired annuities: they include smokers, or people with health problems that generally shorten life, such as obesity and diabetes.

Certain occupations – like physically demanding ones – that are reckoned to shorten life, may also qualify for a higher annuity from some insurers.

Open market option: The only way to find out how much you might receive for your lump sum is by shopping around. This is known as using your open market option (OMO), which means taking up your right to get the best quote for your lump sum that you can instead of simply taking an annuity from your current pension pot provider.

top tip: it is possible to unite the lump sums from various pensions in order to obtain the best price under an OMO.

OTHER ANNUITY OPTIONS

Although pensions can be a highly attractive form of investment because of the tax relief they offer, there is one aspect disliked by many savers: the fact that if they buy an annuity with the pot of money they have saved up, their estate will receive nothing in the event of their death. Or if money is left to the estate, that it will be subject to a heavy Inheritance Tax (IHT) charge. There are ways to reduce this possibility, for example by the use of guaranteed payments (see opposite), although the concern is that by using these options, the annuitant is simultaneously reducing the actual amount of annual pension paid to him or her.

In addition, some people dislike the fact that they are forced to buy an annuity at times when rates may not be as high as they might like. They prefer their money to be invested for longer while still paying them an income. This explains why many annuitants are keen to explore options that allow them to do this.

With-profits annuities

These link income to a with-profits fund. The returns from the underlying investments are 'smoothed' over time to calculate how much the fund pays out. You select your first year's income by choosing an anticipated bonus rate. The higher the selected bonus rate, the higher the initial income. However, recent poor stock market performance means many with-profits policies are paying out less and less.

Unit-linked annuities

Similar to with-profits annuities but do not 'smooth' when times are bad, which means your income may vary. They are not for the faint-hearted.

Income drawdown

Most pension lump sums must be cashed in for an annuity at 75. Before then, you can either defer taking your pension completely, leaving it to grow in your chosen fund or you can go for an income drawdown option. This allows you to continue investing your money, but you also receive an income until the annuity is bought.

The amount of income you take must be within the strict limits set by the Government Actuary's Department, which are about 35 per cent of what you might expect for a single life, level annuity.

The serious risk here is that the stock market can fall – while in the intervening years you have used part of your pot to buy yourself an income. This leaves even less to buy an annuity with when you reach the age of 75.

Phased retirement

This is where you cash in a portion of your pension in stages and live on that income, leaving the rest to be invested until you reach 75, when you are supposed to buy an annuity with the rest of your money. If you die before 75, your estate receives the left-over lump sum.

Alternatively secured pension (ASP)

From the age of 75, it is also possible to switch your remaining pot to an ASP, rather than purchase an annuity. An ASP operates in a similar way as income drawdown, but with some different rules:

You can withdraw 55–90 per cent each year of how much you would be paid with a flat rate single-life pension.
These limits must be reviewed every year.
Regardless of your age, the maximum income will be based on someone's age at 75.
The funds are invested in a similar way to an income drawdown arrangement and are therefore subject to investment risk.
You can convert your ASP into a standard annuity at any time.

In the event of your death, any remaining invested fund value can be used to provide a:

- Spouse, civil partner or dependent's ASP for someone over the age of 75 years, or
- Spouse, civil partner or dependent's unsecured pension for someone under the age of 75 years, or
- Pension annuity for a spouse, civil partner or dependent, or
- Charity lump sum death benefit, or
- Lump sum death benefit (where there is no surviving dependent).

Where unused funds are subsequently used for the benefit of a spouse or civil partner there will be no immediate charge to IHT. However, if on the subsequent death of that person there are still unused funds remaining, those unused funds will be taxed for IHT as if they had formed part of the original pensioner's estate on death.

Women and pensions

Women face far bigger problems than men when it comes to receiving a decent pension at retirement.

On average, today's single women pensioners have an income £24 a week lower than single male pensioners. Unfortunately, many women's employment history works against them. Women working full-time still only earn, on average, about 80 per cent of male full-timers' hourly rate. Women who work part-time earn just 60 per cent. This means their occupational pensions, where available, will be smaller.

Once women reach retirement, they lose out again through lower annuity rates than men, because of their longer life expectancy.

WHAT SHOULD WOMEN DO?

Find out where you stand. To do this, fill in a BR19 form from the Pension Service (see page 214). You can also think about saving more:

Contribute more into your occupational pension through top-up schemes. More details are available elsewhere in this section.

If you do not have enough money, ask your partner to save in a stakeholder scheme on your behalf. If you both survive to an old age and stay together, you and he will both enjoy the benefits of your pension, plus he receives tax relief on the contributions.

If you have gaps in your employment history not connected with caring for relatives or children up to the age of six, you may buy back 'added years' in respect of your pension by making backdated NICs. This will give you a bigger income when you retire. Note that each missing year reduces the basic State Pension by 2–3 per cent.

Take out extra protection. This means your partner having life insurance in place in the event of his premature death, protecting you and your children where necessary. Cover at death is either paid as a lump sum or an annual income for a defined period. More details are in the insurance section (see pages 80–2).

Long-term care

The issue of care for the elderly has grown in importance as more and more people become older – and crucially, as they pass over the threshold of 75 years and realise that they are likely to need help with their daily living.

Unfortunately, the NHS no longer covers all the costs associated with care in old age: that responsibility has been transferred to local authorities, with the NHS normally providing only the nursing and medical component of a person's long-term needs.

SELLING YOUR ASSETS

Currently, care home bills for the poorest are met by the State, but anyone with savings above £22,250 in England and Northern Ireland (£22,000 in Wales, £22,500 in Scotland) pays for long-term care. In most cases, the value of any property owned will be included within this sum. However, there are certain circumstances where the home is excluded:

If the care needs are classed as temporary.
If a surviving spouse or civil partner lives there. This rules extends to other relatives aged 60 or over who live in the property. So if a daughter, niece or brother has moved in as a carer, this could help reduce future care costs.
If it is owned on a tenancy-in-common status. Most couples buy a house as joint tenants. This ensures that on the death of either party their share is automatically transferred to the other, but as tenants-in-common, this gives both parties the freedom to leave their share of the home to whoever they like. If, say, the husband has died and left his share of the home directly to the children, or to a trust, then the value of his wife's share of the property will be ignored if she needs care at

a later date. This is because her half of the home is decreed to be worthless, as it can't be sold on the open market. To effect such a change you would need to alter the deeds to your property, which will cost between £150 and £200.

You could also consider splitting any joint accounts so that only the care home entrant's savings are eroded. But note that if a local authority believes assets have been given away specifically to avoid paying care costs, it retains the legal right to challenge these disposals.

HOW TO PAY FOR CARE
There are three main options.

Deferred option scheme
If your other assets are below the means-test limit, you can ask the local authority to pay care costs and they will place a charge on your property to be paid on your death.

Investment
Many people choose to sell their home and invest the proceeds, using the income generated to help pay care fees. Alternatively, you can let the property with this money raised going towards care. This means your family has to maintain and manage the property. But they may prefer doing so if the alternative is that they lose some of their inheritance.

A care fees annuity
From the proceeds of the sale of your home you can buy an annuity – available from insurance companies – to provide a guaranteed income. This means that the price of care is capped and protects the remaining capital. But for those that die shortly after going into care it could prove a more costly option.

Equity release

In recent years, as increasing numbers of elderly people are finding it hard to make ends meet, more and more are prepared to consider selling a portion of their home while still continuing to live in it. The lump sum is used to provide an income. This is known as equity release. But at the same time, equity release can be a minefield, full of traps for the unwary.

LIFETIME MORTGAGES

This is where the size of a loan available to elderly borrowers is largely based on their age. Interest, which is fixed for the lifetime of the mortgage, is added to the loan and repaid on the sale of the property. Meanwhile, the elderly person retains the right to live in the property until his or her death.

Here is how it works in practice: say you are a 60-year-old. An insurer would offer to lend you up to 17 per cent of the value of your property. A 72-year-old would be offered up to 29 per cent. The different amounts that a company will lend is based on actuarial calculations about your future life expectancy.

So, for example, a home valued at £200,000 might allow someone aged 60 to borrow up to £34,000, or £58,000 for the 72-year-old. Based on a typical current fixed mortgage rate of around 6.8 per cent for an equity release product, the amount owed would double every 11 years. So if the 72-year-old dies aged 83, their debt would be £116,000, leaving £84,000 to their heirs, assuming the property does not increase in value.

HOME REVERSIONS

Here you actually sell a proportion of the property to a company but you retain the right to live in it. The amount offered for that share will not be the existing market rate, but a proportion of it, again based on actuarial calculations of a person's life expectancy.

For example, a 72-year-old might be offered between 45 and 49 per cent of the value of a property. So, on that £200,000 property, a 50 per cent share of the home would mean the seller receiving between £45,000 and £49,000.

In effect, by signing away a proportion of the home for less than it is worth, the customer pays for the product upfront. This may explain why reversionary loans only account for 10 per cent of the market.

Drawdown mortgages: Instead of taking the loan as a single lump sum at the start, you take smaller amounts over time. These amounts can be taken at regular intervals or as and when you need them. Because you are taking smaller amounts over time, the total amount you owe will grow more slowly than if you take a lump sum at the start.

Interest-only mortgages: The loan you get is a cash lump sum. You pay interest on the loan each month at a fixed or variable rate. The amount you originally borrowed is repaid when your home is sold. Note that if the interest rate is variable and your pension or other source of income is fixed, you may find it more difficult to meet your repayments when interest rates rise.

WHY ARE PEOPLE SUSPICIOUS ABOUT EQUITY RELEASE?

Equity release products of one type or another have been available for almost 40 years. But despite the fact that more than £1,000 billion is tied up in property, barely £1 billion worth of equity release plans are sold each year and that figure has remained static since 2003.

There are several reasons for this, and they include mis-selling scandals in the late 1980s, when many elderly homeowners were persuaded to sell part of their homes and invest the money for income – only for interest rates to rocket while stock markets fell.

Do your sums

Generally, experts believe that a home reversion will pay out more to people with a long life expectancy. But if you believe property prices will rise more than 5 per cent a year, then reversion becomes expensive: you are giving up a share in the value of your home, which is rising fast in value.

Today, regulation of the market is far more effective and Safe Home Income Plans (SHIP) acts as an effective trade body for almost all providers in the industry, ensuring higher standards. However, extreme care is still needed when taking out such products.

POINTS TO TAKE INTO CONSIDERATION

If you are interested in equity release, be very careful. Equity release schemes could be expensive, inflexible and leave people with little equity, according to Which?. Furthermore, any money people release from their property could affect the level of means-tested benefits that they were entitled to. For example, an individual needing to move into sheltered housing or a retirement home may have to pay back some of the loan earlier than expected. This could potentially leave them with too little equity to buy a new property. If you are considering equity release, consider the following issues:

Tax. Although the lump sum you receive will be free of tax, any income from that money will be added to your remaining income and taxed. You may lose some or all of your age tax allowance.

Benefits. If you are in receipt of state benefits, you may find that the income you receive from equity release will affect them. You may end up with a smaller income.

Charges. It can cost up to £2,000 to arrange, including legal and valuation fees, plus an arrangement charge.

Maintenance costs. You will have to keep your home in a good decorative state because the provider receives part of its value on death. This can become expensive.

Inflation and house rises. If house prices rise steeply, you or your beneficiaries may have paid a very high price for the scheme.

Your family. Inheritance is a fraught issue and it will help to consult with those who stand to lose some of it.

Your future options. If you want to move house you may not be able to.

Other options. These include downsizing to a cheaper property, using existing savings, or even borrowing money from family that could be paid back when your home is eventually sold.

Finally, always obtain independent financial advice before taking out such a scheme.

9: Property and finance

This chapter is mainly concerned with buying or remortgaging your home – what factors you should consider and what costs are involved – together with other closely related matters.

- **To buy or not to buy?**

- **Taking out a mortgage**

- **Buying costs**

- **Other ways to purchase a home**

- **Tax and property**

To buy or not to buy?

A property purchase is almost certainly the largest single financial transaction most of us are likely to make in our lifetimes. It also involves an enormous emotional commitment.

Moreover, in recent years, a home has often been seen as more than simply a roof over our heads but as a major investment in its own right Had this book been written three or four years ago, it would probably have recommended that you should get your first step on the housing ladder as soon as possible. It is a measure of how times have changed that an argument like this can no longer be made with certainty.

Perhaps the best way of deciding whether this is a sensible financial decision is to look at the pros and cons of buying a home. The first thing to decide is whether you want to rent or buy. There are benefits and disadvantages to both options, depending on your individual situation, but here are a few general issues to consider.

WHY YOU MIGHT WANT TO AVOID BUYING

Property is a depreciating asset: House prices have fallen sharply since the end of 2007 and it is hard to see them recovering quickly. They fell by about 15 per cent in the course of 2008 and many experts were predicting a similar drop in 2009 and into 2010. After the last housing market falls between 1989 and 1994, prices mostly remained stagnant for several more years – with some brief spurts of recovery lasting a few months at a time.

Negative equity: This is where the value of your home falls below the level you paid for it – and especially the amount you have borrowed to buy it. In turn, it means selling a property becomes impossible unless you make up any difference between the sale price and what you owe your lender. Again, after the collapse in 1989, many homebuyers found themselves unable to move for years.

Mortgages are hard to come by: The mortgage market is now effectively closed to most first-time buyers. The best deals are available only to those with deposits of at least 25 per cent and the potential to borrow mortgages worth six or seven times income has gone. Today, almost all lenders work on a multiple of three to four times earnings.

Ownership costs more than you think: There is Stamp Duty Land Tax to consider: this is a tax of 1 per cent on all purchases over £175,000 until the end of December 2009, reverting to £125,000 thereafter. It then rises to 3 per cent on purchases over £250,000 and 4 per cent over £500,000. This amount is payable on the entire sale price. Also, experts suggest that unless you are living in a new-build property, you should set aside 1 per cent of its original asking price each year for basic repairs and upgrades.

WHY YOU SHOULD CONSIDER BUYING

Rent is money down the drain: If you rent a property for 10 or 20 years, you own nothing. If you buy, even if prices stagnate, you still own something.

Historically, property prices rise: There are cyclical falls, such as those experienced in the mid-1970s, the early 1990s or most recently, the long-term movement in prices, which tends to rise over much longer periods of time. For example, according to Nationwide Building Society, a house priced at £10,000 in the first quarter of 1974 would have been worth almost £151,000 in the same quarter 25 years later.

Delaying means you may miss out: Many would-be buyers think they can wait until prices reach their lowest ebb and enter the market at that point. Some may be able to do that. But most will almost certainly not recognise that point and miss out on some of that recovery.

Negative equity is not as frightening as you think: Many people are frightened of owing more than their property is worth. It mostly becomes a problem if you cannot afford to keep paying the mortgage (perhaps because you have borrowed too much), or if you want to sell up and move elsewhere. But in reality, if you have a repayment mortgage and simply keep up with your monthly instalments, you will have paid up to 10 per cent of the capital within five years. Assuming you also paid a 10 per cent deposit on the property, that's a 20 per cent buffer after five years.

Mortgages are not impossible to find: Yes, they are much tougher to obtain than before, but if you have a deposit, they are not impossible to find. It may also be possible to buy jointly with a friend.

Demographics are on your side: In 2006–07, the last available figures, the Government estimated that there were some 200,000 homes added to the total UK housing stock, a large increase on the trend, which is closer to 150,000 a year.

   The Government wants 200,000 homes to be built a year, rising to 240,000 a year by 2016. This is to take into account the expected number of new households, growing at about 220,000 a year. But in 2008, it is estimated that barely 100,000 will be built and as few as 65,000 in 2009. That creates pent-up demand.

You decide how you want your place to look: Renting generally means that you are not able to influence the choice of kitchen or bathroom fixtures and sometimes not even paint colours throughout the property. Buying your own home gives you much more freedom.

Home buying rules

Regardless of when – or whether – you decide to buy, there are three key rules to bear in mind when buying a house:
- Do not treat property as an investment but as a roof over your head. Regardless of whether it rises or falls in value over the next few years, it is your home first and foremost.
- Only buy something you really like. Part of the reason why people feel hard done by if prices fall is that they always treated it as a stepping stone to somewhere better, rather than somewhere they would love living in, no matter what happened to its price.
- Only buy what you can realistically afford. Your mortgage payments should ideally cost no more than 25 per cent of your net monthly take-home pay and certainly no more than 35 per cent. This ensures there is enough left over to pay your other bills, as well as having a reasonable buffer to meet any potential interest rate increases.

Taking out a mortgage

At the end of 2007, there were an estimated 16,000 different mortgages available to UK borrowers. By mid-2009, however, that number had fallen to barely 2,000, as the credit crunch forced lenders to restrict their lending significantly.

TYPES OF MORTGAGE

The first decision you will need to make is to decide whether you want an interest-only mortgage or a repayment one.

Interest-only mortgage

Here you pay only the interest on the loan, not the capital. This type of mortgage can make sense if:

You have a temporary financial difficulty and cannot afford to pay both the interest and the capital on the sum you have borrowed.

Your income is irregular and you prefer to make large, one-off lump sum repayments of your capital.

You have an alternative mortgage repayment vehicle in place; for example, an investment such as an ISA or similar, which you can use to pay off the loan. In the 1980s and early 1990s, many people used endowment-type investments for such a purpose. But their poor performance and the inflexibility means that very few are now sold.

You are expecting a large lump sum at some stage; for example, through an inheritance or even a large redundancy payment.

The danger of interest-only loans is that some borrowers pay back no capital for years at a time.

Repayment mortgage

This is where, in addition to the monthly interest, you are also paying back a proportion of the borrowed capital.

Although potentially subject to interest rate movements, payments remain relatively steady throughout the mortgage's lifetime. As the amount you owe is reduced, the amount of interest charged also falls and more of your monthly payments are used to pay back capital. Over the years, your capital repayments speed up. Repayment mortgages can be a good option if you:

● Can afford to make them regularly
● Prefer the certainty of knowing that your loan will be paid back over a set period.

HOME LOAN OPTIONS

Despite the reduction in types of mortgages, the most basic ones – and variants of them – are still around.

Standard variable rate (SVR)

The SVR moves up or down, depending on the cost of borrowing money for the lender. These costs are theoretically linked to the Bank of England base rate, which means that they should move more or less in tandem with any increases or decreases in that rate.

In practice, one of the side effects of the financial crisis of 2007–08 has been that the Bank of England base rate movements are less likely to influence variable rates charged by lenders. Instead, most tend to look at the three-month London Inter-Bank Borrowing Rate (Libor), the rate at which banks lend money to each other.

Generally, a variable rate mortgage is set at between 1.5 and 1.75 per cent above the base rate so the lender can cover its administration costs and make a profit. However, when the base rate was cut to 0.5 per cent at the beginning of 2009, many lenders placed a limit on their variable mortgages, below which they refused to cut costs.

Most borrowers tend not to take out variable rate mortgages when they first buy a home. They usually end up with an SVR when their cut-price initial deal finishes and often use it as a springboard to move to another deal. The advantage of an SVR at this point is that it is often possible to switch out of one without paying a redemption penalty.

Fixed rate

The rate on this type of mortgage is pegged at a certain level for between two and five years, although shorter and longer fixed periods are available. At the end of the period, the mortgage typically reverts to the SVR, or a variant of it. The advantage of a fixed rate loan is that it allows borrowers to know months, even years in advance what their monthly payments will be. This makes budgeting easier.

Fixed rate mortgages almost always come with redemption penalties for those who end the deal early. Sometimes a penalty for leaving is applied beyond the deal period itself. This applies particularly in cases where a lender offers a loss-leader deal and so needs to recoup its money for one or more years after the end of the fixed rate.

Discount mortgages

A discounted mortgage is similar to variable loan deals, in that it can move up or down in line with base rates. The difference is that the discount is pegged to a rate that is below the variable mortgage rate. For example, a two-year discounted deal might be available at 2 per cent below the variable rate. If that moves, so will the discounted rate.

Discounted mortgages run for periods of between six months and five years, although most on offer are one- to three-year deals. In essence, discounts are loss-leaders: the lender hopes that you will stick around long enough after the deal ends so that it can recoup the money it has laid out to attract you.

They are worth having when interest rates are coming down or expected to come down. But if rates are predicted to rise, fixed rate mortgages are usually the best option. If interest rates are moving up and down sharply, some discount mortgages may have a cap or a collar, or both: this is where the rate is guaranteed not to move up beyond a certain level (the cap). Equally, it won't fall below a certain point (the collar), or it may stay be pegged within certain levels – a cap and collar.

Tracker mortgages

A tracker mortgage is a variant of an SVR in that it is linked to the base rate set by a central bank, almost always the Bank of England. It is usually pegged at a certain percentage rate above base.

Trackers first became common in the mid-1990s as a response by some lenders to complaints from borrowers that they were failing to respond quickly to the Bank of England base rate cuts and keeping the cost of their SVRs higher than they should be. By linking their mortgage rates to the base rate, lenders aimed to defuse the issue.

Until 2008, a tracker rate was typically set at between 1.5 per cent and 2 per cent above the base rate, thereby allowing the lender a certain margin to cover administrative and marketing costs, plus make a profit on the deal. However, tracker mortgage providers now have margins reaching 3.5–4 per cent above the base rate in some cases. This makes them far less of a good deal, especially when many experts began to predict that as the economy begins to recover, base rates are likely to rise sharply.

In addition, lenders set collars, a level below which they will not cut mortgage payments no matter what happens to the base rate.

In order to make trackers more attractive when rates are thought likely to be heading upwards, many lenders have started to offer borrowers the opportunity to lock into a fixed rate if interest rates rise. If you think interest rates have fallen as far as they are going to go, or are in danger of going up again, you still have the option of fixing.

Flexible mortgages

A flexible mortgage is a relatively recent innovation that has grown in popularity. Unlike most other types of loan, where the monthly payment is set out in advance for a given period, in this case you have the relative freedom to pay in as much or as little as you want.

A flexible mortgage means that potentially you are able to pay off your home loan more quickly than previously agreed. Alternatively, if times are hard, you can reduce the amount you pay each month, although to reduce your payments for a time you usually have to be in 'surplus' with your lender, having already paid in more than the notional monthly amount. You can often get back payments that have already been made, by agreement with the bank.

Most flexible mortgages use daily interest calculations to work out how much you owe, so every payment is instantly credited against what you owe and the interest you are required to pay falls more quickly.

Bank account or offset mortgages

With this type of home loan, the mortgage is linked to your bank account. Everything you pay in every month is used to reduce the loan, immediately cutting the amount of interest on the capital still owed. So, for example, if you have a mortgage of £100,000 and you pay in a net monthly salary of £2,000, this is offset against what you owe and you only pay interest on £98,000. Of course, as the amount in your current account is spent over the course of that month, the notional amount of interest charged on your overall debt starts to rise again.

With an offset mortgage you actually transfer a proportion of your bank account money into a separate mortgage 'pot'. Although the two pots – the current account and the mortgage one – are grouped together when calculating interest on the overall debt, this method ensures some discipline is applied to your mortgage repayments.

Often you can borrow back money you have already paid into your mortgage account, which can help if you want to carry out home improvements.

WHAT TO LOOK OUT FOR IN A MORTGAGE

Although taking out a mortgage can seem straightforward, there are potential pitfalls. Whether you are buying or remortgaging, here are some things to bear in mind when comparing various mortgages.

Application and completion fees

A typical mortgage fee can reach as much as £1,500, sometimes more. Some of the lowest-priced deals will actually charge a percentage of the loan, up to 3 per cent. This sum is almost always added to the total loan you are borrowing, which means that you will be paying interest on it for the duration of the mortgage period: in effect, over 25 years a £1,500 completion fee can cost between £3,000 and £4,000, depending on the interest rate in place at the time.

High fees are often applied to mortgage deals where a very low rate of interest is being charged. In effect, the trade-off is between a lower monthly payment and a higher overall amount of interest paid over the lifetime of that mortgage.

top tip: deals with high application fees are not generally suitable for first-time buyers and usually only worthwhile if the amount you are borrowing is extremely high.

The most effective way to work out the cost of a high fee is to divide the cost between the period of the deal itself. This is because as soon as the deal ends, you are likely to be switching to another mortgage offer – but the added fee will, by then, be part of the overall amount owed when the new loan is applied for. So, for example, a two-year fixed rate with a £900 fee is effectively costing you an extra £37.50 a month in charges (900 divided by 24), spread over those two years.

Annual or daily interest calculations

With annual interest, your capital repayments – and the interest you must pay on the sum still outstanding – is calculated every year.

With daily interest, each capital payment instantly reduces the amount you owe – and therefore the interest payable.

Most lenders now operate a daily or monthly interest calculation, which means you pay significantly less interest over the lifetime of the mortgage. If in doubt, always ask.

Compulsory insurance

Sometimes a particularly cheap deal is available only if you take out home and contents cover or even life insurance with the lender. Some experts have suggested compulsory home and contents cover can add the equivalent of between 0.25 and 0.35 per cent to the cost of a deal. (For more about home and contents insurance, see pages 185–8)

Mortgage payment protection insurance (MPPI)

MPPI covers you against accident, sickness and unemployment and is discussed on pages 88–9. Again, this is offered by lenders to protect your mortgage payments to them, but if you believe you need this kind of cover and are prepared to shop around, similar cover is often available for less elsewhere.

Redemption penalty periods

If you switch your mortgage to another lender during the lifetime of a special deal, or for a stipulated period after it ends, you may have to pay a penalty.

Depending on how attractive the original offer was and how far into the redemption period it is, this can be anything up to six months' interest. Alternatively, the amount levied is calculated as a proportion of the amount borrowed. So if you take out a £100,000 fixed mortgage with a 3 per cent redemption penalty within the first two years and want to redeem it early, you might be charged £3,000 for doing so.

If this is something that does not appeal, look for deals without redemption penalties, or ones that only apply for the period of the deal itself. Look for offers where the redemption penalty is stepped down: for example, if you leave in year one you pay 3 per cent, dropping to 2 per cent in the second year and 1 per cent in the final year of the deal.

REMORTGAGING: ISSUES TO CONSIDER

Many of the questions that apply to mortgages affect new borrowers and those who are remortgaging. But if you are an existing homeowner looking for a better deal there are two specific issues to consider.

If you are able to borrow a new mortgage

Many homeowners who bought their properties in the period immediately before prices dropped sharply at the end of 2007 may find that they are in negative equity or close to it. In this situation, either their loan to value (LTV) will not allow them to find a very good new deal or they may even be in negative equity, making it almost impossible to obtain a new mortgage, other than at very high rates of interest.

If such a strategy is financially worthwhile

To work that out, add up the potential costs involved and compare them to the total savings from the new mortgage deal.

For example, say you have a £120,000 loan over 25 years, on which you are paying an SVR of 5.29 per cent, your monthly repayments are £730.20. You are offered a two-year fixed rate charging 4.24 per cent, before the mortgage reverts to that lender's SVR. In this case, monthly payments would be £656.45, a saving of £73.75 or £1,770 over the lifetime of the deal.

But what if you had to pay some or all of the following charges?

- Application fee of £800, but can be higher
- Solicitors' fees – up to £400
- Surveyor's valuation fees – about £250
- Redeeming the old mortgage (this is purely the administrative charge, not a penalty) – up to £200.

This means any savings from the better deal are offset by the charges you pay. In some cases, however, your new lender may contribute or meet some of these charges. Also, lenders may allow you to include some of these fees in the new mortgage you are taking out. So if you are just looking to reduce your monthly mortgage payments, it may still make sense to switch to a new deal. But bear in mind that you will be paying interest on them for the duration of the loan.

Alternatively, you could ask your existing lender if there are better deals available as this would help cut overall costs and would also reduce the overall hassle of trying to switch lenders, although there may still be fees to pay.

When not to remortgage

Although remortgaging is a sensible strategy for many borrowers, it may not suit everyone. Here are some people for whom remortgages make little or no sense:

You have only two or three years to go before you have paid off your loan. The amount left to pay is so small that the charges for doing so will never be offset by the savings.
Irrespective of how long you have before the loan is paid off, the amount you owe is small. Again, the savings are likely to be miniscule.
You have a deal with hefty redemption penalties.
You want to borrow more because your finances are in a mess. Unless you have a lot of financial discipline and have now learnt how to manage your finances, you would probably be better off sorting out the mess first: borrowing more money is not a panacea for every problem.

LEASEHOLD AND FREEHOLD

One of the things many buyers encounter when they are buying a property, particularly in urban areas and especially for flats, is the issue of leasehold or freehold.

Freehold means that you fully own the property and you have full responsibility for the maintenance and repairs of the property.
Leasehold means that you own the property for as long as is specified in the lease and are granted the right to live there by the freeholder. You also pay a ground rent to the owner of the land (the freeholder),

usually a small amount paid each year. At the end of the lease, the property becomes the possession of the freeholder.

The majority of leasehold properties are flats, although some houses, particularly in the north of England, are leasehold. The lease sets out who is responsible for maintaining and repairing different parts of the property and any conditions you must meet as a resident. Leases on new properties are typically granted for up to 999 years, but existing leases on properties are usually shorter, often for periods of 100 or 120 years.

Generally, it is not considered advisable to buy a property with a lease of less than 60 years, certainly not for first-time buyers without a large deposit. This is because as a lease runs down to the end of its term, a property's value may actually decrease as it becomes increasingly difficult to sell on and provides less security of tenure to the next buyer.

top tip: leaseholders have the right to extend the lease for 90 years or to buy the freehold if certain criteria are met. Doing so is expensive and you will need advice.

Buying a leasehold property

- Read the lease document carefully and find out how the property is managed. Look for when and how the service charges should be paid and how the charges are split among the tenants.
- Check what the service charge covers: cleaning, heating and lighting of common areas; building insurance; interior and exterior maintenance; reception or security staff – if relevant – and upkeep of grounds or lifts, if there are any.
- Check if there is a sinking fund, which is a charge levied to cover large expenses at some future date, for example, a new lift or painting the outside of the property every few years. The absence of such a fund may seem cheap, but could mean a much larger hit when the time comes for repairs.
- Check whether you or the freeholder is responsible for the exterior of the property. Find out if there is a tenants' association or a management company and if there is, what rules they apply to fellow tenants.

Buying costs

When you are buying a property there are a range of expenses that you will have to meet, both before and after a purchase.

SURVEYOR'S VALUATION FEES

There are effectively three levels of report.

Basic mortgage valuation

This is the most basic of the three. Its main purpose is to confirm that the property is suitable for a mortgage and represents adequate security for the lender. It provides a general description of the property and its condition, together with an indication of the market valuation and insurance value. This report is for the benefit of the lender not you. A valuation is likely to cost between £200 and £300.

Homebuyer's report

This is more detailed than the valuation report. Its aim is to provide the potential homebuyer with details of any major faults apparent at the time of inspection, especially if these are likely to have a detrimental impact on the value of the property. The report will also recommend other surveys that may be necessary, such as a timber and damp report. Unlike the basic report, the valuer acts for you.

   Because the homebuyer's report is much more comprehensive than the basic valuation report, the cost is also higher: £400–£500 plus VAT for an average family home.

Full structural survey

Also known as a building survey, this should provide an extremely comprehensive property report, listing all faults, both major and minor. The surveyor will probably spend three to four hours at the property and the report will run to anything up to 20 pages. Generally, a structural or building survey is strongly recommended for any property

Down-valuations

The property market downturn has led to the possibility of what has become known as 'down-valuation', when a lender values your home at less than you expected, reducing the amount that you can borrow. When a borrower comes to remortgage, lenders assess the value of the property either by using an automated valuation model (AVM), which uses sales data and house price indices to estimate the value of your home, or by sending a valuer to visit the property.

If you believe your intended purchase has been valued at less than its 'real' value, you must provide two pieces of evidence to back up the claim, such as a recent sale in the preceding three months. You could also pay for a second valuation, typically costing £200 to £300, but before pushing for your property to be revalued check with two or three estate agents in your area to ensure there is comparable evidence that the property is worth what you think.

more than 100 years old, of unusual construction or where there have been a lot of alterations or extensions to the property. It is also advisable for expensive properties. A typical structural survey can cost up to £1,000 plus VAT.

OTHER FEES

The survey isn't the only cost you will incur when buying a home.

Lender's application/completion fee

As discussed earlier in this chapter, this cost is now about £1,000 for a reasonably good deal. The fee is usually levied at completion and is generally added to the cost of the mortgage itself.

Mortgage broker's fee

A broker can be useful, in that he or she should know the market well and can probably source a mortgage for you more easily than you could do yourself. This is especially the case for people with poor credit scores. However, the broker's fee can be up to 1 per cent of the mortgage amount – although, typically, the final amount payable can be negotiated back to between £250 and £500. The advantages of using a mortgage broker include the facts given overleaf.

Knowledgeable and in a position to advise dispassionately between wide selection of different providers' mortgages, possibly including some exclusive deals.

Able to steer you in the direction of a lender most likely to consider your personal circumstances in the best possible light.

In a position to handle a lot of the bureaucracy and chase the lender on your behalf.

Possibly able to save enough money from the cost of your loan to make up any fee the broker may be charging you.

On the downside, the broker may:

Be biased towards the commissions paid by some lenders.

Not always be as competent as you might hope for.

Have a far smaller selection of mortgages than you think, perhaps because the company's panel of lenders is not industry-wide.

Try to sell you other products linked to a mortgage to offset the cost of the advice or, failing that, charge a large fee for his or her services.

If you are confident that you understand mortgages, have a good credit rating, can put down a large deposit and are prepared to research the market thoroughly, you almost certainly don't need a broker.

Solicitor's fee

This can be up to £600, plus any disbursements – the costs incurred by solicitors in carrying out their work, such as photocopying, postage, couriers – and other costs. When you are looking for a solicitor to handle your property transaction, there are a number of questions you need to ask.

1 What are your fees?

2 What do your charges include? Most solicitors do not include disbursements in their fees. There will be separate local search fees, possibly an environmental search fee, plus Land Registry charges, probably a bank transfer fee when your money is moved to the other solicitor's account and office copy deeds. Make sure the charge includes faxes and phone calls.

3 Is your firm a specialist in conveyancing work? If a solicitor is not experienced in this area of work, it could mean both delays in the purchase, as well as possible mistakes.

4 How quickly are you able to move to exchange and then completion? You need someone who can focus on your work and get it done quickly. The average period from start to finish should be in the region of six to eight weeks. If you want it done quicker, you must ask first and make sure the vendor's solicitor understands this.

5 Can you give advice on related legal matters? There are times when you want other advice, such as making wills if you are buying a property jointly.

6 What happens if things go wrong? Check if they have an internal complaints system. It is rare for anything too bad to happen on a simple property transaction and you will almost certainly want to take the complaint outside the firm if you don't get redress internally. But knowing that they have a system in place can give you peace of mind.

STAMP DUTY LAND TAX (SDLT)

This is a tax levied by the Government on all property purchases. Note that SDLT applies to the entire amount you are paying on the property, not just the element above the particular thresholds. For example, a £250,001 home will cost £7,500.03 in SDLT.

SDLT exemptions

In December 2006, Chancellor Gordon Brown announced that newly built zero-carbon homes will be exempt from SDLT until September

Stamp Duty Land Tax

Property value	Duty payable
£0 to £175,000 (until 31 December 2009 when reverts to £125,000)	0%
£175,001 to £250,000	1%
£250,001 to £500,000	3%
£500,001 or more	4%

2012. Homebuyers are also exempt from paying SDLT if the home they are buying costs less than £500,000 and is carbon-neutral. Environmentally friendly properties costing more than this get a reduction of up to £15,000. But you must have a zero-carbon home certificate from an accredited assessor to qualify.

MORTGAGE PAYMENT PROTECTION INSURANCE (MPPI)

For many mortgage borrowers, making sure their monthly bills are paid regardless of whether they fall ill or become unemployed is vital, particularly in the current economic crisis – this is discussed on pages 88–9).

HELP AGAINST REPOSSESSION

Since January 2009, faced with an increased number of people whose homes risked being repossessed because they could not pay their lenders, the Government decided to revamp its rules to provide more help for homeowners through Homeowners Mortgage Support.

If you are receiving Income Support, income-based Jobseeker's Allowance or income-related Employment and Support Allowance, you will now be entitled to support on your mortgage interest payments (not the capital) after 13 weeks. Previously the waiting time was 39 weeks for new claims or in some cases 26 weeks.
You can claim help on loans up to the value of £200,000, or the first £200,000 of a larger loan. The rate at which interest can be paid on such a loan is fixed at 6.08 per cent until December 2009, when it will be reviewed.

Note that there are strict eligibility criteria. For example, if you are out of work but your partner is still in a job, the amount paid towards your mortgage interest will depend on his or her earnings. For more information, go to www.direct.gov.uk.

In all such cases, if you find that you are in financial difficulties, one of the first, and most important, things you should do is contact your mortgage lender and work with them to find ways of ensuring that you can stay in your home until you find new work or, if you have been ill, are able to resume your job.

HOME AND CONTENTS INSURANCE

One of the more significant annual bills most of us have to pay when we buy our own home is that of buildings and contents insurance. In almost all large urban areas around the UK, the cost of both types of insurance – one broadly protects the fabric of a home, the other covers possessions inside it – averages about £500 a year.

Despite its cost, it is virtually impossible to buy a home without at least taking out home insurance, as distinct from contents protection. Mortgage lenders make it a condition of their loans that such cover must be in place – home insurance safeguards not only your interests but theirs as well, at least until you have made the final payment on your mortgage.

Home insurance is a potential minefield: many people pay too much for their cover, or else they discover, usually too late, that the protection they thought they had was not up to the job. So how should you approach taking out home and contents cover? There are two points worth noting:

Although often sold as a single package, the two types are separate. It often (though not always) makes sense to buy them separately.
In many cases, home or contents insurance offered by your lender is unlikely to be the best value, particularly if offered as a condition of a seemingly cheap mortgage deal. Always shop around.

Premiums

These are based on a combination of factors:

The value of the house and its contents. Typically, this is defined less as the purchase price of the home itself, or even its current value, but how much it would cost to rebuild.
Its postcode. People living in inner-city areas often pay more because insurers believe there is a higher risk of burglary and/or vandalism.
The type of property. As above, homes of unusual construction are more expensive to insure, partly because of the added risks involved, such as thatched cottages.
Individual claims history. This is pretty obvious: the more you claim, the more you pay.

Levels of cover

A basic policy will cover you for a series of specified risks. These include storms, fire, lightning, explosion, subsidence, thieves and vandals. But it is often sensible to make sure that the policy also covers frost damage to pipes and accidental damage to underground pipes and cables.

Moreover, damage to a home – and its contents – often happens by accident, often caused by the occupier. Cover against such damage, for example a ruined carpet, or accidents to wallpaper and furniture, is usually a sound move.

Remember that in the event of a fire, for example, you will be suffering damage that may need to be claimed from both home and contents insurance at the same time. Your kitchen units, for instance, should be covered as a 'fixed item' under a home contents policy, because they are generally anchored to a wall. But a freestanding cupboard might not be.

Exclusions

Most policies have standard exclusions, things for which you are not covered, so ensure you read the small print. Such items may include the costs of routine wear and tear, deliberated damage by the insured party (you, that is) and smoke damage. Check, too, if there are limits on the amount that can be claimed for specified valuable items, such as

---

Choosing a contents policy

When taking out a contents policy, you have two main types to choose from.

New-for-old. If your belongings are stolen or damaged beyond repair, the policy will pay for the cost of a brand new replacement. This may not mean you will be given the money to buy what you want. More and more insurers replace items themselves.

Indemnity cover. This gives you the current value of your items, often a fraction of the replacement cost. Such policies are often cheaper, but potentially risky in the event of a major burglary or serious damage, such as a fire. Note too, that underclothes and linen are covered only on an indemnity basis even under most new-for-old policies.

electrical goods, jewellery and works of art. For any single items over a specified value, check with the insurer if they will be covered.

How much cover?
The sums you insure for are generally based on two approaches: bedroom-rated or sum-insured.

Bedroom-rated policy: Your premiums are based on the number of bedrooms in your house, although it does not restrict claims to the value placed on the rebuilding cost of an individual room or replacing its contents. Generally, the valuation is generous enough to ensure that that you are amply covered. However, such policies are sometimes slightly more expensive.

Sum-insured policy: You have to calculate the value of your home and its contents yourself. The advantage is that you set down exactly how much all your possessions are worth, the potential rebuilding cost and the replacement of fixed items. The disadvantage is that the process is more time-consuming. Also, you risk under insuring your home: any claims may then be scaled down by the proportion by which you are unprotected. For example, if your home is worth £200,000 and you only insured it for £100,000. A fire then causes £100,000 of damage. Your insurer will only pay out £50,000, half the cost of the policy.

Cutting the cost of the cover
Generally, you pay the first £50 or so of every claim yourself, known as a compulsory excess. However, you may also have the choice of higher excesses in return for which, the insurer will reduce premiums.
Don't claim for small losses. No-claims discounts are becoming increasingly common.
Loyalty discounts are given for staying with an insurer for a long time. But don't ignore that fact that shopping around may be cheaper.
Don't ignore insurance brokers. Many brokers can offer policies that are competitive, as well as more closely matching your specific needs. You can often get them to cut the cost of their quote by telling them that you have obtained a cheaper one elsewhere – they simply sacrifice some of their sales commission. Don't try to lie, however: they know the cost of cover and they will simply send you on your way.

Key points to note

1 Always shop around. Insurers rely on inertia for their profits. They know that most people will tend to stick with one provider for several years at best, indefinitely at worst. You should aim to get a better deal on your home and contents every two years.

2 Utmost good faith. All contracts between an insured party and an insurer are based on this notion. It means you have a duty to disclose any information that may affect the granting of a policy or its cost.

Insurers take this point extremely seriously and one of the biggest stumbling blocks for would-be claimants often turns out to be a small piece of information they discover should have been passed on at the time of taking out the cover.

3 The small print. Insurance varies widely not just in price but also in scope. For example, there will be exclusions on the amount paid out for individual items, or a minimum standard of security for your home may be required. If in doubt, speak to an insurance broker: peace of mind is always worth a few pounds extra.

4 Don't over insure. Many people will take out cover that protects them against thefts from their car. Yet they also have all-risks home contents cover, which would protect their possessions while in transport. Or they may take out cover that is already provided through their work: life insurance is one example, where many employers pay three or four times an employee's salary on his or her death.

5 Don't under insure. It may seem ironic to say this, given the above advice, but many people manage to do both, as with the earlier example of sum-insured policies.

6 Documents. Never be caught out without your policy immediately to hand. If the policy is related to your home or your health, keep it somewhere safe – and where it won't be damaged. You may need to use it.

7 Always keep records. If disaster strikes, receipts will be vital in obtaining full compensation for whatever is lost.

Other ways to purchase a home

There are other, less conventional, routes you can take to purchase a home, ranging from buying at auction to renting at a reduced rate prior to buying the property.

BUYING AT AUCTION

When people find it difficult to sell a property, they resort to auctions. The advantage of an auction is that as long as the reserve price is low enough, sellers are guaranteed to find a buyer for their home within a few minutes. For buyers, there are both advantages and disadvantages. Here are some of them:

The pros
- No need to deal with estate agents
- It is just you against other buyers
- The sale is legally binding. The vendor can't change his or her mind
- It is very quick: you can end up owning a property within 28 days, having exchanged contracts days earlier
- You could end up with a bargain. In September 2008, the average price of the 3,993 homes sold at auction between June and August was 23 per cent lower than the same period a year earlier. The price drop was far greater than for properties sold through estate agents.

The cons
- It can be a daunting experience
- Sometimes the pre-auction period is not long enough to carry out in-depth checks on the property
- You can't change your mind once you have won the bidding

- The temptation is to pay too much because people get carried away by the atmosphere of the auction itself
- Unless you have lined up a loan and a lawyer who can expedite everything speedily after the auction ends, you could be in trouble.

The basic rules for buying at auction

Attend a few auctions, soak up the atmosphere and get a sense of how the bidding works and the ways people compete.

Contact all auction houses selling properties in the areas you're interested in and ask for their catalogues. Some will have the details online, so be prepared to do a few searches.

View one or more properties.

Ask yourself why the property is being sold at auction. It could also be that the seller wants to get rid of it quickly. It could also be that the property is unsellable by other means.

Unless you can spot things like damp, poor wiring, dry rot, subsidence and a myriad other major structural problems that may affect the property, pay for a surveyor to go round and prepare a report for you. This is particularly important if you are later hoping to persuade a lender to offer you a mortgage on a property.

At the very least, take round a skilled builder who can give you an idea of how much it will cost to bring the property to the right standard. Then add a few thousand pounds to that estimate.

RENT TO BUY

For many would-be buyers, uncertain about proceeding at a time when the property market is stagnating, the option of trying out a property before buying it can seem attractive. If so, there are a number of schemes available that aim to help.

New Build HomeBuy

This is a government-backed venture aimed at first-time buyers who earn up to £60,000, but can't afford to buy a property to suit their basic household needs in the area where they live or work. Priority is given to social tenants and public sector key workers. The Government buys up unsold developers' properties stock. The idea is that you will be able to rent a new-build home with a view to buying it within a set period (around three years).

The rent is set at 80 per cent of the market rent, or less, to allow you to save for a deposit. At the end of the defined period, as long as you can pay the deposit and your circumstances haven't changed for the worse, you can buy a share in the property. You buy 25–75 per cent of your home on shared ownership terms, and pay an affordable rent on the rest. You would also have the option, as you become able to afford it, to buy additional shares until owning 100 per cent.

Details were announced at the end of 2008, but the first pilot scheme had yet to take off by the summer of 2009, so it is difficult to say how successful it is likely to be. But there are some potential downsides to it.

If you can't proceed with the purchase at the end of the term, your tenancy may not be renewed and you may have to move out.

If you own less than 100 per cent of the property, you would have to sell it to another household nominated by your landlord.

Private schemes

Many private developers are keen to encourage people to buy. They are unveiling schemes based on permutations of the following:

Tenants pay a monthly rent, which they get back at the end of the one or two years' contract, giving them between 5 and 10 per cent towards their deposit.

If you buy a property within the first six months of starting to rent, they will refund 100 per cent of the rent towards your deposit. Buy within 12 months and you get back 75 per cent of the rent, buy within 18 months for 50 per cent back, and, if you buy within two years, you get back 25 per cent. Rent is set by local letting agents and the sale price is set when you are ready to buy, at which time a valuation is carried out.

If either of these schemes appeals, draw up a list of properties that meet your needs and would be happy to buy, and approach the estate agent or private seller with a proposal on how it would work.

The potential downside here is that, until you actually complete the purchase you are a tenant and, as such, there will be limitations on how you use the property. Also, make sure it is clear whether you are agreeing the sale price at the beginning of the contract or at the end, as either have potential advantages and disadvantages.

KEY WORKER LIVING PROGRAMME

The Government is also making money available through housing association umbrella groups, enabling more homes to be built that can be jointly owned by housing associations and first-time buyers.

The Key Worker Living programme is targeted at workers in key occupations, such as nurses and other NHS staff, teachers, social workers, police officers and fire fighters, who live in London, the south and east of England, including parts of East Anglia, and are unable to afford to buy.

The system works by allowing members of key groups to borrow up to £50,000 on an interest-free loan and add it to whatever they borrow when buying a property of their own choice or when purchasing a newly built home from a housing association. Financial help is available not just to first-time buyers but also those who may already own a home but need help to buy a larger one because their family has grown. In addition, some London teachers recognised as potential leaders in their schools can apply for interest-free loans of up to £100,000. When they sell their home, this loan must be repaid.

Under this scheme, when a property is sold, the lender gets its money back, plus a proportional share of any increase in the value of the home. People who leave their job will usually have to pay back the money within two years.

BUYING WITH OTHERS

Buying a property together with friends or family has both advantages and disadvantages. It can boost your purchasing power, allowing you to find somewhere nicer than you might have been able to afford on your own. You share the cost of the deposit, purchasing fees, ongoing mortgage repayments and household bills.

On the minus side, there is a danger that you and your friend or family member might not be compatible as housemates and that you may be left holding a share of a property you cannot afford or with bills that are not yours but for which you are now liable.

If you are planning to buy together with someone, you need to work out all the details first. These include:

- How much each of you will put in as a deposit
- How legal and other purchase costs will be met

SDLT when sharing with others

It is not unheard of for friends to buy together but when one person wants to move, he or she must offer to sell their share to the other housemate. In such cases, a buyer could be left with an extra SDLT bill. If you buy someone else's share in the property for more than £175,000, you will be liable for 1 per cent of that amount in tax. Above £250,000, the amount you would have to pay in stamp duty rises to 3 per cent, or £7,500 (see page 183).

- How the bills will be paid, including mortgage, insurance and utilities
- Who takes responsibility for cleaning and keeping the place tidy
- What happens if one person needs to move out and/or sell up and the other one does not.

There will also be the cost of a cohabitation agreement between you, where issues such as privacy, noise and guests staying over, are discussed and all parties sign legal documents referring to each of these points. You may also need to take out life insurance to cover your side of the mortgage if anything happens to you.

Legal forms of home ownership

If you are buying jointly with someone else, make sure the purchase contract sets out the right form of joint ownership.

Joint tenancy: Under this version, neither party can sell their share of the property without the other's agreement. If one party dies, the other automatically inherits the other's share. This is suitable for adults buying a property as a couple, but less so if you are buying with a friend.

Tenancy-in-common: Under the terms of this arrangement, each party can sell on his or her share, either while still alive or through a will. This is much more suitable for friends buying a property together when they don't intend to live together as a couple.

In Scotland, joint tenancy or tenancy-in-common does not apply, although the law is similar. A property can be held in joint names by stating in the title deed (using a survivorship clause) that each of you will leave the property to the other if one of you dies.

Tax and property

Unlike some other assets that can be held in tax-free wrappers, like ISAs or personal pensions, homeowners are not always able to shield their properties against tax. That said, there are some exemptions that are worth noting, both in relation to your own home and also with regard to second and buy-to-let properties.

But first, where does the law stand? There are three main taxes that you need to be aware of: Capital Gains Tax, Income Tax and Inheritance Tax.

CAPITAL GAINS TAX (CGT)
Many people assume that CGT is something that only applies to the better-off. After all, when was the last time that anyone made capital gains of more than £10,100 (the limit for 2009–10), in any tax year? In fact, it is easy to find oneself facing large CGT bills, especially if you own a second property and sell one of them.

At its simplest, CGT is payable if you sell something for more than you paid for it. Buildings, land, shares, part of a business and expensive antiques or jewellery are the sorts of things that usually attract a CGT liability. However, you may also have to pay CGT if you simply give something away or receive compensation or prize money.

On the other hand, you do not have to pay CGT if you are selling or otherwise passing on personal belongings that are worth less than £6,000, or if you give assets to a registered charity. Nor is it payable when selling your private car and your main home, or when you receive money from ISAs, Premium Bonds, betting, lottery or pools winnings, or personal injury compensation. You do not have to pay tax on gains below £10,100. Above that, the rate of tax payable is 18 per cent.

Property exemptions

As with all taxes, there are ways to reduce your CGT liabilities. One of them is by taking advantage of various exemptions that apply to the CGT rules that relate to property.

For unmarried couples: Each can nominate a home as their main residence, even if it is used as a weekend place. Transferring the second home into your children's name is also possible.

For married couples: Joint ownership offers two potential CGT allowances instead of one. It is also possible to nominate which of two properties will be the second home. Buyers have two years from the date of purchase to inform their tax office in writing. Unless the second home is of higher value and would incur more CGT if sold, it makes sense to nominate the home you live in.

Three-year relief: Where a property may only intermittently have been a main residence – perhaps because it was occasionally rented out, or maybe the owner had another property that was chosen as a main residence – any gain on disposal must be apportioned on a time basis between both homes.

Again, there is a loophole: apart from the factual period of main residence, the last three years of ownership of a property are also treated as though it was the main residence, even though it may not have been.

For example, increasing numbers of people buy a property, live in it for a year or so, then buy another and move out while still renting out the original one. Clearly, the first one is no longer the main residence. But if you sell within those first three years, CGT would not be due because that period of ownership is treated as though the property were the main residence.

The three-year relief can work in other ways. Say the letting lasts for five years after you move out and then you sell. In this case, the exempt period would be the first year because you were living there, plus the three years for the relief, compared with the total ownership of six years. So, on selling, only part of the gain would become taxable.

This would be calculated by multiplying the gain by one third – the two years' ownership not covered by the main residence exemption.

Where a gain is made on disposal of a property that has been a main residence at some point, but has also been let as residential accommodation, a further relief on gains up to £40,000 is available.

The rules that say you don't have to pay CGT

If you transfer a property to your spouse or civil partner when you are living together, you won't have to pay any CGT on the property at that time. However, your partner may have to pay CGT when the property is sold. You also don't have to pay CGT when you sell or dispose of your home as long as all of the following apply:

It was your only home for the whole period you owned it (ignoring the last three years you owned it).
You used it as your home and nothing else all the time you owned it.
For the whole period you owned it, you didn't let any of it out or didn't have more than one lodger.
The garden and area of grounds sold with it, including the site of the house, is no more than 5,000 square metres (about the size of a football pitch).
You bought it – and made any improvements to it – to use as your home rather than to make a gain.

If you meet all these conditions, you are entitled to private residence relief and won't have to pay CGT. You can only claim private residence relief on one home.

When you first buy a property, you may still be able to get the full relief if you can't move into a property immediately when you first buy it – for example, you can't sell your old home or you need to refurbish the property. If you move in within 12 months, you will still get the full relief. This may be extended to two years in exceptional circumstances.

You will still get the full relief if you couldn't live in your home because you were working away and all of the following apply:

You were working abroad (or you were working in the UK and absent for four years or less).
You lived in the property both before and after you went away.
You had no other home that qualified for private residence relief.

Business asset exemptions

For many people CGT is something they are likely to face when disposing of their businesses. Indeed, the sale of a business is treated by many self-employed people and small traders as being a key part of their pensions. Since 6 April 2008, individuals have been able to claim relief on the first £1 million of gains made on the disposal of all or part of a business, or a disposal of a business's assets after a business has ceased. The relief gives an effective rate of 10 per cent on all qualifying gains up to £1 million. Claims can be made on more than one occasion up to the £1 million lifetime limit. Gains over £1 million are charged at 18 per cent.

CGT planning

Here are some further ideas to consider to help potentially reduce your CGT bill.

Offset losses against gains: If you hold a range of assets, such as shares, there is a possibility that you may have recorded losses on some of them. In this case, consider disposing of assets that have shown a loss at the same time. You can set it against a taxable gain.

Maximise tax-free gains: Everyone, including children, has the same CGT allowance. Spread ownership of your investments to maximise your tax-free gains.

Transfer assets to your spouse or civil partner: CGT allowances apply to individuals: therefore married couples and civil partners receive two sets of allowances. You can effectively double your tax-free allowance by giving assets to your spouse to dispose of. Gifts between a husband and wife who are living together are deemed to take place at initial cost rather than the current price, and are ignored for the purposes of CGT.

Defer the gain: If there are no losses or reliefs you can use to cut your tax bill, you can defer it by reinvesting the gain in an Enterprise Investment Scheme (see page 48), buying shares in small companies that are trying to raise venture capital to grow their businesses. However, this can be a potentially risky path and you should avoid investments purely for tax purposes.

Bed-and-breakfast your gains: The old system, whereby you used to be able to sell assets and buy them back the next day to avoid CGT on long-term investments, is now outlawed within 30 days of the original sale. But you can still mimic the old bed-and-breakfast arrangement by selling the assets and getting your spouse to buy an identical holding, immediately buy a similar asset or buy an option to protect against a price increase over that 30-day period.

Get professional help

If you believe you are likely to be affected by CGT in any way, you should consult a tax expert. To find a chartered accountant who can advise on tax issues see page 215.

INCOME TAX

Letting residential investment property is treated as running a business, even if you only let out one property. If you let out more than one property in the UK, they will all be treated as a single business. So, whether you let one or several properties, you are taxed on the overall net profit. This is worked out by:

- Adding together all your rental income
- Adding together all your allowable expenses
- Deducting the allowable expenses from the income.

Working out your net profit like this means that you can offset a loss from one property against the profit from others. Your net profit counts as part of your overall taxable income.

The deductions that are generally allowed by HMRC include:

- Mortgage interest (but not capital)
- Insurance costs
- Rates
- Cost of decorating/repairs
- Wages and costs of services.

Rent-a-Room scheme

If you are letting furnished accommodation in your home to a lodger and your total receipts (rent plus income from meals, laundry services) are £4,250 or below, you can receive this Income Tax free under the Rent-a-Room Scheme. You will have to pay tax on anything over £4,250.

Let your home

If you let your home while you live somewhere else, your profits are worked out and taxed in the same way as for residential investment lettings (see Income Tax, opposite). The same rules apply if you let part of your home outside the Rent-a-Room Scheme. If you let part of your home this way, you can include a percentage of household costs like gas and electricity when you work out your allowable expenses.

The tax rules for furnished holiday lettings in the UK are different from the rules for residential lettings. The rules allow you to:

Reduce your profit by claiming capital allowances for the cost of furniture and fixtures that you provide inside the property you let.
Offset any losses against your overall income, not just against your rental income.

Also, when you sell the property you may be able to take advantage of extra reliefs that will bring down your CGT bill.

How to reduce your income tax bill as a landlord

Although you are liable to pay Income Tax on the rent you receive, there are legitimate ways of reducing your income. Here are five tips that can help you do that.

Claim large costs as revenue costs rather than capital: If you can class a cost as a revenue cost, it will improve your cash flow as you will pay less property Income Tax. For example, if you have had a new conservatory built or a new bedroom added, this is clearly a capital expense because it has increased the value of the property.

However, sometimes distinguishing between the two costs is not so clear. If you currently have rotten single glazed windows, then you will be able to replace them with UPVC double glazed windows and offset the entire cost against the rental income. There will be no need to class this as a capital cost. You can do this because it is generally accepted that the standard windows used in modern properties are UPVC and not wooden single glazed windows. So you are replacing the current standard window fitting with a like-for-like window.

Claim tax relief on all expenditure: If you have incurred a revenue expense on your property, then you can offset it against the rental income. This includes costs incurred when travelling back and to the investment property; advertisement costs; telephone calls made (or text messages sent) in connection with the property; the cost of safety certificates; bank charges; advisory fees, such as legal and accountancy; even subscriptions to property investment related magazines, products and services.

Make sure you register any rental losses: It is not a compulsory requirement to register your losses with HMRC. But doing so will help you save tax: by registering these losses with HMRC you can offset them against future profits. This means you are reducing your tax liability going forward.

Switch property ownership with your spouse or civil partner: If you have a spouse or civil partner who is a lower or even nil-rate taxpayer and you are a higher-rate taxpayer, consider moving the greater portion of the property ownership into his or her name. This means that a greater part of the profit will be attributed to him or her, reducing your tax liability.

Mix and match your Wear and Tear Allowance: If you are offering a fully furnished property, you receive a 10 per cent Wear and Tear Allowance on furniture and other items in it. Alternatively, you can claim a Renewals Allowance when you next get round to replacing damaged items. You can start to claim the relief as soon as you start to receive income from the property. So if you have bought a property in the last 12 months and have fully furnished it, it may be better to start using the Wear and Tear Allowance because you will be providing high-quality

top tip: if you sell the property before renewing the furnishings, then by using the Renewals Allowance, you will not be able offset any renewals cost against your property.

furnishings and will not expect to replace them for five or even ten years. By claiming the 10 per cent Wear and Tear Allowance you will be able to start claiming the relief immediately.

INHERITANCE TAX (IHT)

IHT is essentially a form of death duty – a tax charged on what you leave behind when you die. Another way of looking at is as a fee levied by the Government when you leave your wealth to your heirs.

Until ten years ago, IHT was not much of an issue. Ironically, it was the property market boom from the late 1990s that has changed things. Property prices trebled in many parts of the UK between 1997 and 2007, putting millions of people over the IHT limit and making their estates subject to tax when they die.

Although only 5 per cent of estates being settled today are over the current IHT limit, it is the future application of the rules – when today's generation of homeowners pass away – that has left many people concerned.

IHT is calculated by valuing all the estate's assets, deducting any liabilities, then deducting the nil-rate band, which is £325,000 in 2009–10 (£350,000 in 2010–11). Whatever is left is taxed at 40 per cent. Any IHT is then paid by the estate's executors before they are able to hand over the inherited assets to the beneficiaries.

IHT planning

With a bit of planning, it is possible to reduce the eventual size of your IHT bill.

1 Use the seven-year rule. You can gift money or other assets to anyone you like and, if you survive for seven years after the gift, it becomes a potentially exempt transfer (PET) and no IHT is paid on it.

If you die before that time, your estate pays IHT on a sliding scale, ranging from the full amount in the first three years to 20 per cent of the total bill in year six.

To minimise the effect of death inside those seven years, you can take out a decreasing life insurance policy on the person who made the bequest. This pays out a sum of money over those seven years, equal to the IHT bill you would face. You or your parents can also use PETs to gift the entire estate, including the main property. But if the former owner wanted to keep living in the property, they would have to pay a full market rent over those seven years.

2 Make a will. This is not just for peace-of-mind reasons: apart from anything else, if you are cohabiting, your partner is not automatically entitled to any part of your estate. More importantly, a will is the key mechanism for reducing tax payable after death.

Many couples have their wills structured so that all assets are passed to the surviving spouse or civil partner, who is automatically not liable to pay IHT. But when that person dies, HMRC will be back. The most common way of reducing your IHT bill, therefore, is to set up a trust, which is simply a written arrangement whereby an appointed person is given assets to hold and manage for the benefit of those named in the trust deeds.

Solicitors and accountants are experts in using trusts to help cut people's tax bills. Discretionary trusts are a case in point: take an estate valued at £1m and set up a nil-rate band discretionary trust.

Then, divide your assets before death so that each spouse has half. This includes property, which can be done by registering yourselves as tenants-in-common instead of being joint tenants (see page 193).

When one partner dies, the other already has £500,000 on which no IHT is paid. The remaining £500,000 can then be split two ways: £325,000, the nil-rate band limit, goes into a discretionary trust for the children or relatives, while the rest goes to the surviving spouse or civil partner.

This basic scheme means that on the survivor's death IHT will ultimately be paid on assets of £675,000, minus her own estate's £325,000 nil-rate band, a total of £350,000. The tax on this would be £140,000, a saving of £130,000 if the trust had not been set up.

Even if a discretionary trust has not been established by the time of death, the survivor has a two-year window to create a deed of variation, changing the terms of their deceased partner's will to benefit their children.

Moreover, the trust mechanism can be complex and some solicitors argue that the time and costs involved in administering a trust are disproportionate to the advantages unless an estate is worth a significant amount of money, as the tax saved can be offset by other costs. But while they may no longer be necessary for joint estates of less than £650,000, discretionary trusts are of great importance in other circumstances. Nil-rate band planning can still be used regularly to ensure:

Access to funds by the surviving partner.
Interest-free loans can be made to the surviving partner repayable on his or her death, further reducing the IHT liability.
That the assets held in trust are not assessed as capital of the surviving partner should he or she require long-term care.
That the trust assets pass to your children rather than your spouse's new partner, should he or she remarry.

3 Take out life insurance. Set up a life insurance policy to pay out on your death. The policy is set up in trust and is for an amount equal to the amount your estate might otherwise be liable for. Generally, premiums on these policies are paid by those who stand to benefit from your will.

4 Make lifetime gifts. Some gifts are exempt from IHT because of the type of gift or the reason for making it. These include:

Wedding gifts/civil partnership ceremony gifts (to either of the couple), which are exempt from IHT up to certain amounts. Parents can each give £5,000, grandparents and other relatives can each give £2,500, and anyone else can give £1,000. You have to make the gift on or shortly before the date of the wedding or civil partnership ceremony. If it is called off and you still make the gift, this exemption won't apply.
Small gifts. You can make small gifts, up to the value of £250, to as many people as you like in any one tax year (6 April to the following 5 April) without them being liable for IHT. But you can't give a larger sum: £500, for example, and claim exemption for the first £250. And you can't use this exemption with any other exemption when giving to the same person.
An annual exemption. You can give away £3,000 in each tax year without paying IHT. You can carry forward all or any part of the £3,000 exemption you don't use to the next year but no further. This means you could give away up to £6,000 in any one year if you hadn't used any of your exemption from the year before.

Combining lifetime gifts

You can't use your annual exemption and small gifts exemption together to give someone £3,250. But you can use your annual exemption with any other exemption, such as the wedding/civil partnership ceremony gift exemption. So, if one of your children marries or forms a civil partnership, you can give them £5,000 under the wedding/civil partnership gift exemption and £3,000 under the annual exemption – a total of £8,000.

Case study

Ray Peters, aged 45, and his partner Rhiannon, 38, own a three-bedroom property now valued by local estate agents at £365,000 (in 2007, the value was £475,000). Their combined annual income is £125,000 (both are in the 40 per cent higher tax bracket), and still owe £135,000 through an offset mortgage on the property, with a current SVR of 3.7 per cent. They can withdraw up to £300,000 in accelerated repayments on their existing mortgage.

The couple, who are not married and have no children, want to buy a larger home and rent out their existing one, if possible, until the property market recovers in a few years' time. They have been told they can expect up to £1,600 monthly rent on their existing home. They also want to know how to shelter their current and future purchase from tax, as well as avoiding a large Inheritance Tax bill in the future.

Goals
- Buy a new property.
- Rent out the existing property.
- Shelter the proceeds against tax.

Plan
- Because their jobs are steady and they have no other major outgoings, Ray and Rhiannon can possibly borrow up to four times their combined income. This would allow them a maximum mortgage of up to £500,000, on which payments at 5 per cent would be £2,956 a month. If they can find up to 25 per cent of the purchase price, another £165,000, they could afford a home priced at £665,000.
- If they scale back their demands and look for something currently priced at £450,000, they could reduce their deposit to just over £112,000, while their

5 Give gifts as a part of your normal expenditure. Any gifts you make out of your after-tax income (but not your capital) are exempt from IHT if they are part of your regular expenditure. This would include monthly or other regular payments to someone, including gifts for Christmas, birthdays or anniversaries, and regular premiums on a life insurance policy (for you or someone else). Keep a record of your after-tax income and your normal expenditure, including gifts you make regularly. This will show that the gifts are regular and that you have enough income to

borrowings would fall to £337,000. Or they can increase the deposit as a proportion of the purchase price: a lower loan-to-value gives them the option of finding a better mortgage deal and also has tax advantages (see below).

- The couple can rent out their existing property for £1,600 a month. That would meet the repayment cost of a £275,000 buy-to-let mortgage on their existing home, although the fee would be very high: up to £3,000 for some deals. Or they could take out an interest-only mortgage, which would come to £1,145 a month, assuming a rate of 5 per cent. By pushing their borrowing up from £135,000 to £275,000 on their old property, Ray and Rhiannon are freeing up a deposit for the new property they wish to buy.
- A mortgage broker should be able to use the couple's combined work-related and rental income to negotiate a suitable mortgage package.
- Ray and Rhiannon can offset rental costs against the income they receive from the property. Crucially, this includes mortgage interest: the higher the mortgage interest payments on the rental property, the less tax they pay. So it makes sense for their broker to find a lender willing to offer as big a mortgage as possible on their rental property so as to increase the deposit they put down on the new home instead.
- If the couple want – and if it meets current safety regulations – they can leave their existing furniture in the property and claim a 10 per cent Wear and Tear Allowance on it. If they sell within three years of renting it out, the old property will be exempt from CGT as it was Ray and Rhiannon's primary residence before it became a rental property.
- If the couple want to avoid IHT problems in the event of either of them dying, the simplest solution would be to get married, as married couples pay no IHT on what they inherit after the death of their spouse.

cover them and your usual day-to-day expenditure without having to draw on your capital.

6 Give maintenance gifts. You can also make IHT-free maintenance payments to your spouse or civil partner, your ex-spouse or former civil partner, relatives who are dependent on you because of old age or infirmity and your children (including adopted children and stepchildren) who are under 18 or in full-time education.

Probate, IHT and falling prices

Ironically, one of the concerns of some people in the past year or two has been that the recent collapse in property prices means they might be paying too much IHT on an inherited estate. This is because IHT is based on valuation at time of death not the actual price achieved when the property is sold.

It is possible to appeal against the original value of the estate because of an inflated property value. If so, this must be done within four years of the date of death, by presenting additional evidence that the eventual sale was made on the open market for a lower figure. To do this, an executor must obtain and fill in form IHT38, which can also be downloaded from HMRC website: www.hmrc.gov.uk.

top tip: if the sale price of an inherited home is lower than its original valuation at the time of probate, you can apply to pay less IHT by filling in form IHT38.

Glossary

Administration Order
A court order whereby you make a monthly payment to the court, which then distributes that money on a pro rata basis among your creditors. The court takes 10 per cent of your payment as handling fees to cover costs.

Annual percentage rate (APR)
The interest rate for a whole year (annualised), rather than just a monthly fee/rate, which is applied on a loan, credit card, mortgage or overdraft. An APR of 15 per cent means a loan of £1,000 will involve repayments of £1,150 over a year.

Annuity
A financial contract that pays an income. When linked to a maturing pension, the income is paid for life.

Assets
A collection of different investments that make up a person's portfolio.

Bond
Either an IOU, usually issued by a company, which promises to pay a fixed rate of interest for a certain number of years, at the end of which the debt will be paid back. Or another name for lump sum investments, usually issued by banks or insurance companies.

Child Tax Credit (CTC)
A tax-free saving scheme designed to help parents, relatives and friends save on behalf of their children. It is backed by the Government, which makes two payments of at least £250 each (one at birth, the other at age seven). The CTC matures at 18.

Collective investments
A collection of share-based assets, or similar, professionally managed in a fund rather than being bought individually by an investor.

Commutation factor
The relationship between the lump sum taken and pension given up. The more lump sum you take out of your pension pot, the less annual income you receive.

Correlation
A situation where different types of assets – shares, fixed interest investments and so on – are affected differently by changes in the economy. Negative correlation is where there is little or no connection between assets and changes in the economy. Positive correlation is where different assets move in tandem with each other.

County Court Judgement (CCJ)
A judgement that a county court issues when someone has failed to pay money that they owe. It is a way for creditors to claim the money they are entitled to. In Scotland, they are known as Decrees.

Disabled Person's Tax Credit
An additional payment, made through the UK tax system, to people who are disabled and in paid employment for at least 16 hours a week.

Enterprise Investment Scheme (EIS)
A government scheme that provides a range of tax reliefs for investors who subscribe for qualifying shares in qualifying companies, generally small and higher-risk.

Equities
A share of stock in a company.
Equity-based investments
Investments that are based on shares in companies.

Feeder account
An account that allows you to temporarily 'park' money that you later want to transfer into other savings schemes.
Fixed-rate bond
An investment, lasting between three and ten years (usually five or six years) that pays savers a fixed rate of interest, as income or added to the bond. At maturity you receive the original investment back.

Income Support
A government benefit paid to people who are on a low income and working less than 16 hours a week. This can include someone who is sick or disabled, lone parents responsible for a child under 12 years of age, carers or registered blind.
Individual Savings Account (ISA):
A tax-free savings or investment account that allows up to £10,200 (after April 2010) to be invested into it every tax year, of which £5,100 can be in a cash account.
Individual Voluntary Arrangement (IVA)
A legal contract between debtors and creditors, enabling them to pay off their debts over a fixed period, subject to the agreement of those they owe money to.
Investment trust
A fund whose manager invests in a variety of different company shares or other assets. Unlike other types of collective investment, the trust itself is a publicly quoted company, whose shares can be bought and sold on the stock market.

Jobseeker's Allowance (JA)
The main benefit that is paid to people who are out of work. It is linked to a person's previous Class 1 National Insurance contributions, which means that self-employed people generally do not qualify for this benefit.

London Inter-Bank Lending Rate (Libor)
The interest rate that the banks charge each other for loans, also a reference point for the rate that lenders levy on their fixed rate and variable mortgages.

Mutual funds
Another term for 'collective' funds, such as unit or investment trusts, which are professionally managed and can hold dozens of different shares, corporate bonds and other assets.

Negative equity
When the value of your home is worth less than the mortgage owed on it.

Pension credit
A means-tested benefit that tops up pensions to a guaranteed minimum amount.
Personal or stakeholder pension
A long-term saving scheme where you save money into a pot. The scheme benefits from generous tax relief by HMRC on contributions. At retirement, the lump sum is used to buy an annual income for life, also known as an annuity.

Share
A certificate representing one unit of ownership in a company or mutual fund, or limited partnership.

Stock

Strictly speaking, it is the capital raised by a company through the issue of shares that entitle holders to an ownership interest (equity); 'he owns a controlling share of the company's stock'. Also a more generic term used to describe equity holdings (for example, a stocks and shares ISA).

Standard variable rate (SVR)

A mortgage rate that is not fixed but which can rise and fall in line with other economic factors, such as Bank of England base rates or the London Inter-Bank Lending Rate (Libor).

Tax wrapper

A way to describe an investment that is treated in a particular way by HMRC. For example, investing in a fund will receive different tax treatment depending on whether the wrapper is a pension or an ISA.

Total expense ratio (TER)

The total annual cost to an investor of managing a fund or collective investment. This includes the managers' own annual charges as well as other expenses, such as trading fees, legal fees, auditor fees and other operational expenses.

Tracker

Either a fund that replicates the performance of a stock market index, such as the FTSE 100, or a mortgage whose charges are linked to the Bank of England base rate.

Unit trust

A fund whose manager invests in a variety of different company shares or other assets. Investors are issued with 'units', whose prices rise or fall in line with the underlying investments in the fund. When they sell up, those units are cancelled.

Venture Capital Trust (VCT)

A VCT is designed to encourage investment in small unquoted companies. Individuals invest by holding shares in a VCT. The VCT invests in a spread of small unquoted companies, enabling investors to spread their risk, just as they do by holding shares in an ordinary investment trust company. If the VCT is approved by HMRC, investors enjoy substantial tax reliefs.

With-profits funds

A type of pooled investment fund, normally offered by insurance companies or mutual societies. They generally offer some life insurance cover. They invest in a combination of shares, property, cash and bonds. Investors' funds receive annual bonuses, usually less than the fund's overall performance. When the fund matures, a terminal bonus is added on top. Insurers claim this allows them to 'smooth' both growth and losses, so there are no wild swings in performance from year to year.

Working Tax Credit (WTC)

A tax credit paid through HMRC to working families who are responsible for at least one child under 16 (or under 19 if in full-time education up to A level or equivalent standard). The applicant or partner (if they have one) must be working 16 hours or more per week.

Contacts and links

Any book such as this one will inevitably only scratch the surface in terms of providing all the information you may need to manage your finances efficiently. Luckily, the internet is a wonderful way of getting extra help. Here are some websites (and telephone numbers) for a variety of organisations and services that have lots of easy-to-understand material you can access at any time.

1: FINANCIAL GOAL SETTING

Directgov: The Government's website also has a section on financial goal setting. Go to www.direct.gov.uk and key 'goal setting' in to the search box.

The Financial Services Authority's (FSA) Moneymadeclear website offers the option of a financial health check. You can find out more here: www.moneymadeclear.fsa.gov.uk/tools.

2: PLANNING YOUR FINANCES

If you know your way round the internet even just a little, you will almost certainly have come across the websites from the main newspaper groups in the UK. All of them carry content from their personal finance sections, published in the weekend or midweek. In some cases, they carry additional online content too. Here are some of the main newspaper sites:

Financial Times: www.ft.com
The Guardian: www.guardian.co.uk
The Independent: www.independent.co.uk
Mail and The Mail on Sunday: www.thisismoney.co.uk
The Telegraph: www.telegraph.co.uk
The Times: www.timesonline.co.uk

Here are some additional sites with good material:

MSN Money: http://money.uk.msn.com/
Yahoo Money: http://uk.finance.yahoo.com/

To find out more about how to contact a financial adviser, go to the Moneymadeclear website, at: www.moneymadeclear.fsa.gov.uk/products/advice/financial_advice.html.

3: MAXIMISING YOUR EARNINGS

Directgov has lots of useful information about employment rights, rates of pay, holiday entitlements and so on. They can be found here: www.direct.gov.uk/en/Employment.

HM Revenue & Customs (HMRC) is the best source on all tax-related information. Although some of the content on its website can seem complicated, much of it is written in an easy-to-understand way. Go here: www.hmrc.gov.uk.

4: CREDIT AND DEBT

Citizens Advice: A network of advisers across the UK who are able to help with debt-related issues, as well as negotiate on your behalf with creditors. Go to: www.citizensadvice.org.uk.

Consumer Credit Counselling Service: The UK's leading debt charity offers advice to those in financial difficulties. Go to www.cccs.co.uk or call 0800 138 1111 to speak to a debt counsellor.

Credit reference agencies: There are three leading credit reference agencies who hold masses of information about you. This information is used to determine your status when you apply for a loan or any form of credit. You can 'repair' any misinformation held about you by contacting each company (see pages 55–7).
CallCredit: www.callcredit.co.uk
Equifax: www.equifax.co.uk
Experian: www.experian.co.uk

Data sharing: Debate and in-depth sharing of data you know about is a cornerstone to the ability to make good financial decisions. Several excellent websites allow you to do that. They include:
Interactive Investor: This was one of the earliest web-based financial information sources. It focuses heavily on share price information, but also has some great savings comparison tools. It can be found at www.iii.co.uk.
MoneySavingExpert: Billed as the 'consumer's revenge' website, it has many hundreds of thousands of active members who share tips and warnings about dodgy dealers. You can find it at www.moneysavingexpert.com.
MotleyFool: The term refers to a jester from the Middle Ages, the 'wise fool' who both instructed and amused, and could speak the truth to the king without getting his head chopped off. The website has lots of interesting material and can be found at www.fool.co.uk.

Insolvency Helpline: This is a privately funded body paid for by accountants and legal experts operating in this sector. But it has a mass of great information and additional links that you may find useful, especially on bankruptcy as well as IVAs. Go to www.insolvencyhelpline.co.uk/.

MoneyMadeClear: The FSA's consumer help website, has information about loans as well as credit reference agencies. Go to www.moneymadeclear.fsa.gov.uk.

National Debtline: A charity providing impartial advice to people across the UK who are facing debt problems. Go to www.nationaldebtline.co.uk or call 0808 808 4000.

Office of Fair Trading (OFT): This is the regulator for loan providers, controlling who gets consumer credit licences. They set the rules whereby credit should be provided. Go to www.oft.gov.uk for more information or call 08457 22 44 99.

Price comparison websites: Nowadays it is possible to get a much better deal on a range of financial products by shopping online. Here are some financial comparison websites that can tell you which products are best for you:
CheapFlights: Good resource for finding and booking the cheap flights anywhere. Can be found at www.cheapflights.co.uk.
Confused.com: Well-known insurance comparison site. Can be found at www.confused.com.
Flightcomparison.co.uk: Another flight comparison service: www.flightcomparison.co.uk.
GoCompare: A comparison website

for insurance and other products – www.gocompare.com.

MoneyExpert: Linked with Defaqto, a company that provides statistics to the FSA. Can be found at www. moneyexpert.com.

Moneyextra: Was one of the first comparison sites to float on the stock market but has since been bought and sold many times over. Can be found at www.moneyextra.com.

Moneyfacts: One of the oldest price comparison services. Can be found here www.moneyfacts.co.uk.

Moneysupermarket: Probably the widest range of price comparisons, everything from savings accounts to utilities and even payday loans. Can be found at www.moneysupermarket. com.

Skyscanner: Claims to search over 600 airlines on 200,000 routes to 5,000 airports. Can be found at www. skyscanner.net.

Travelsupermarket: Part of the same company as moneysupermarket.com. Allows you to compare flights, hotels rooms and vehicle hire. Can be found at: www.travelsupermarket.com.

uSwitch: Started out helping people to find different utility providers, but has since branched out into many other areas. Can be found at www.uswitch. com.

Which?: The leading unbiased reviewer of financial products and provider of information on everything from mortgages to cars to computers. It can be found at www.which.co.uk or call 01992 822800.

5: PROTECTING YOUR FAMILY'S FINANCES

Association of British Insurers (ABI): Represents the insurance industry: www.abi.org.uk or call 020 7600 3333.

British Insurance Brokers Association (BIBA): This is the trade body for brokers who specialise in selling general insurance. Its members are supposed to be experts in obtaining cover for all sorts of unusual insurance needs. It offers a postcode search system for a broker near you: www.biba.org. uk or call the consumer helpline on 0870 950 1790.

That said, if you only need basic cover, you should be able to find it more cheaply from a price comparison website.

Financial Services Authority: The City's leading financial watchdog, can be found at www.fsa.gov.uk or call 020 7066 1000.

Financial Ombudsman Service: Where to go if you have a complaint about a financial provider or an adviser. Can be reached at www. financial-ombudsman.org.uk or call 0845 080 1800.

Jobcentre Plus: This is the Government's organisation that provides help and advice on jobs and training for people who can work and financial help for those who cannot. Go to www.jobcentreplus.gov. uk or call 0800 055 6688. If you live in Northern Ireland, go to the Incapacity Benefits Branch at www. dsdni.gov.uk or call 028 9033 6000 or the benefit enquiry line on 0800 243 787.

MoneyMadeClear: This is the FSA's consumer information website. It includes advice on how to buy insurance and what questions to ask, as well as a jargon buster. You can find more details at: www. moneymadeclear.fsa.gov.uk.

Office of Fair Trading (OFT):
Enforces consumer protection law and competition law. Can be found at www.oft.gov.uk.

6: BUILDING UP SAVINGS

Compound interest: Remember when we were talking of how interest added to interest means that the value of your savings can rise much faster than you think? Try it online with any sum of your choice by going to www.link42.co.uk.

MoneyMadeClear: The FSA's website has an interesting section on savings accounts, along with a fantastically useful comparison tool: www. moneymadeclear.fsa.gov.uk//hubs/home_savings.html.

7: INVESTMENTS

Association of Investment Companies: Represents many investment trust managers and has useful fact sheets and other data you can use. Go to: www.theaic.co.uk or call 020 7282 5555.

Association of Private Client Investment Managers and Stockbrokers: This website carries information on where to find a stockbroker as well as answers to some frequently asked questions about stockbrokers: www.apcims.co. uk or call 020 7448 7100.

Citywire: A new twist on the fund rating system, which looks not to much the fund itself but the manager who looks after it. This is because fund managers are like footballers: they switch companies often, making it difficult to assess the long-term future of a fund itself. More details can be fund at: www.citywire. co.uk.

Compare and find a stockbroker: for an informative account on where to find and how to deal with a stockbroker, use this service from the MotleyFool financial website: www. fool.co.uk/brokers/information/choosing-a-broker.

Ethical Investment Association: A group of independent financial advisers who promotes ethical investment. Go to: www. ethicalinvestment.org.uk or call 020 7749 9950.

Ethical Investment Research Service (EIRIS): This is the leading body promoting ethical finances as well as investigating companies' ethical, environmental and social policies and performance. You can also find details of independent advisers who can help with ethical financial products. Go to: www.eiris. org or call 020 7840 5700.

FT Fund Ratings: the *Financial Times'* highly regarded rating system for funds, which assesses them on the basis of charges, performance, risk and individual assets held in the fund. Its service is available here: http://fundratings.ft.com/fundratings/.

Investment Management Association: Lots of interesting information on funds investing both in the UK and outside, including the sectors they are in. Go to: www. investmentuk.org or call 020 7831 0898.

Lipper Fund Intelligence: A website that allows users to look at both fund performance and charges, using the more accurate and reliable total expense ratio (TER). You can access it at: www.lipperweb.com.

Morningstar UK: Another great source of online fund-related information for investors, available at www.morningstar.co.uk.

Trustnet: For up-to-the-minute statistics on how funds are performing, go here: www.trustnet.com.

Understanding investment risk: Some excellent advice from the consumer advice website Which? can be found here: www.which.co.uk/advlce/understanding-investment-risk.

8: PENSIONS

The Guardian newspaper has an online calculator (http://money.guardian.co.uk/calculators) that can help you work out how much to save, based on how much of a pension your monthly contributions will buy you.

The Pensions Advisory Service (TPAS): An independent non-profit organisation that provides free information, advice and guidance on the whole spectrum of pensions, including state, company, personal and stakeholder schemes. Can be reached at www.pensionsadvisoryservice.org.uk or call 0845 601 2923.

The Pensions Regulator: The watchdog for UK occupational pensions schemes: www.thepensionsregulator.gov.uk or call 0870 606 3636.

The Pensions Service: If you ever want to know anything about state pensions, including what you may be entitled to when you retire, here is a website to go to:

www.thepensionservice.gov.uk. You can also establish the value of your combined state pensions by filling in form BR19 online or calling 0845 300 0168.

9: PROPERTY AND FINANCE

British Association of Removers: Represents the UK's top 500 removal firms. As with other trade bodies, they operate a code of conduct, insurance against damage (which you pay for) and also offer a search facility to find a removal firm near you. There is also a conciliation service if things go wrong. You can find them on www.bar.co.uk or call 01923 699 480.

Council of Mortgage Lenders: Represents the home loans industry, which means it has a mass of statistics about loans, prices and other research into buying habit. Inevitably, its comments will be skewed in favour of its members' interests, but it is a highly intelligent body and always has something interesting to say. It can be found here: www.cml.org.uk or call 0845 373 6771.

Directgov: For an overview of your rights, plus many helpful links to other websites where you can get more advice, visit www.directgov.org.uk/homeandcommunity. Among the many sections there is one on renting.

HousePriceCrash: A few years ago, no one believed house prices could fall. Only a few people, mostly grouped around this website, thought the property market's rise was not inexorable. Although there appears to be a significant degree of self-interest and wish-fulfilment at work by some of its contributors, it is no more biased than an estate agents' website would have been two or three years ago.

It carries a lot of useful information and links to other websites. Go to www.housepricecrash.co.uk.

Institute of Chartered Accountants in England and Wales (ICAEW): Should you need to find an accountant, go to this website: www.icaew.com. The website for the Institute of Chartered Accountants of Scotland (ICAS) is www.icas.org, and for the Institute of Chartered Accountants in Ireland (ICAI) go to www.icai.ie.

National Association of Estate Agents (NAEA): Describes itself as the UK's 'leading professional body for estate agency'. Its 10,000 members, both in the UK and overseas, are bound by rules of conduct, which in theory make them more ethical than counterparts who refuse to join the NAEA. The trade body also has the power to discipline its members. You can check whether the agent you are dealing with is an NAEA member by going here: www.naea.co.uk or call 01926 496800.

NewBuild HomeBuy: to find out more about this scheme, go to www.housingcorp.gov.uk or call 0845 230 7000.

Ombudsman for Estate Agents (OEA): An independent service for home buyers, sellers, tenants and landlords. Operates a code of practice for agents and adjudicates on complaints against them. Its website has some useful information on your rights and how to complain: www.oea.co.uk or call 01722 333306.

Index

**Which? is the leading independent consumer champion in the UK.
A not-for-profit organisation, we exist to make individuals as powerful as
the organisations they deal with in everyday life. The next few pages give
you a taster of our many products and services. For more information, log
onto www.which.co.uk or call 0800 252 100.**

Which? magazine

Which? magazine has a simple goal in life – to offer truly independent advice to
consumers that they can genuinely trust – from which credit card to use
through to which washing machine to buy. Every month the magazine is packed
with 84 advertisement-free pages of expert advice on the latest products. It
takes on the biggest of businesses on behalf of all consumers and is not afraid
to tell consumers to avoid their products. Truly the consumer champion. To
subscribe, go to www.which.co.uk.

Which? Online

www.which.co.uk gives you access to all Which? content online and much,
much more. It's updated regularly, so you can read hundreds of product reports
and Best Buy recommendations, keep up to date with Which? campaigns,
compare products, use our financial planning tools and search for the best cars
on the market. You can also access reviews from *The Good Food Guide*,
register for email updates and browse our online shop – so what are you
waiting for? To subscribe, go to www.which.co.uk.

Which? Legal Service

Which? Legal Service offers immediate access to first-class legal advice at
unrivalled value. One low-cost annual subscription allows members to enjoy
unlimited legal advice by telephone on a wide variety of legal topics, including
consumer law – problems with goods and services, employment law, holiday
problems, neighbour disputes, parking tickets, clamping fines and tenancy
advice for private residential tenants in England and Wales. To subscribe, call
01992 822 828 or go to www.whichlegalservice.co.uk.

Save and Invest
Jonquil Lowe
ISBN: 978 1 84490 044 2
Price: £10.99

Save and Invest is a detailed guide to all saving and investment avenues suitable for those approaching the markets for the first time and those seeking to improve their portfolio. Jonquil Lowe, an experienced investment analyst, introduces the basics of understanding risk and suggests popular starter investments. Many types of savings accounts are closely analysed, along with more complex investment options, such as venture capital trusts, high-income bonds, hedge funds and spread betting.

Money Saving Handbook
Tony Levene
ISBN: 978 1 84490 048 0
Price: £10.99

From low-cost air travel and zero per cent finance to cheap mobile phone tariffs, the list of financial products is endless and the good deals are harder to find. Personal finance expert Tony Levene separates the cons from the bargains and explains how to avoid hidden charges and penalty fees. *Money Saving Handbook* is the key to becoming smarter with your money.

Managing Your Debt
Phillip Inman
ISBN: 978 1 84490 041 1
Price: £10.99

Managing Your Debt is a practical and straightforward guide to managing your finances and getting your money, and your life, back on track. Phillip Inman covers a wide range of topics including how to identify and deal with priority debts, the best way to make a debt-management plan, who to contact and what to expect should you ever face bankruptcy or an individual voluntary agreement.

Which? Books

Which? Books get to the heart of subjects that really matter. We offer impartial, expert advice on savings and investments, pensions and retirement, property, making the most of your money and major life events. As the job market stumbles, we have advice on CVs and interviews and how to turn your idea into a thriving business.

For some light relief and recreation, we also publish the country's most trusted restaurant guide, *The Good Food Guide*. Every year we bring you the latest reviews, foodie features and top tips for budget eats. To find out more about Which? Books, visit www.which.co.uk or call 01903 828557.

"Which? tackles the issues that really matter to consumers and gives you the right advice and active support you need to buy the right products."